A Note About Safety

Although the methods I demonstrate in *How to Build Anything* are considered safe practice in the woodworking industry, the responsibility for working safely ultimately rests on your shoulders. As a result, the publisher of this book (Grassland Publishing and EZwoodshop.com) assumes no responsibility for damages, injuries suffered, or losses incurred as a result of following the information that is presented in this book.

Remember that power tools can be especially dangerous. Spend time with your owner's manual to learn how a tool operates, the safety features included with that tool, and any other information the tool manufacturer thinks you should know before using that tool. This book is intended to supplement the owner's manual, not replace it.

Also, it's your responsibility to protect yourself against the potential health hazards of working with wood. That means using protective eye wear (safety glasses, goggles), ear protection (plugs, earmuffs), and dust control products (respiratory masks and dust filters). Also, if fatigue, stress, or other physical problems are affecting your best judgment, stop working and return to the shop on another day.

Don't let impatience and carelessness ruin the fun!

Andy Duframe

About the Author

Andy Duframe is the creator of www.ezwoodshop.com and owner of Grassland Publishing, a company devoted to helping independent authors. For more information, please visit: www.ezwoodshop.com

Learn More: Building Wood Projects

If you like what you see in *How to Build Anything,* visit my website for more how-to guides, building techniques, and wood project ideas:

www.ezwoodshop.com

This book is dedicated to my loving and supportive wife of twelve years.

How to Build Anything
Contents

✂---- **BOOK CUTOUTS**

Pages marked with this symbol
are designed to be cut from this
book for use in the shop.

how to build anything
3 Tools

Tools for today's DIY builder are small, lightweight, and super easy to handle.

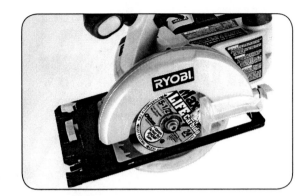

Circular Saw

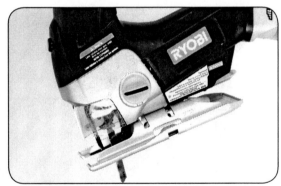

Drill / Driver

Jigsaw

the small-shop workhorse
Circular Saw

Tough and dependable, a circular saw handles the grunt work of cutting boards with ease.

Know these Controls

Trigger
Most saws include a safety thumb lock—a feature that keeps you from accidentally starting the motor when you pick up the saw.

Blade Depth
Blade depth makes a big difference in the quality and safety of a cut. See page 7 for some important tips on how to set blade depth.

Bevel
Beveled cuts are nice for some projects, but don't trust the printed numbers on your saw. Check for accuracy on a scrap piece of wood.

Why a Circular Saw?

The first step in building any project from wood is getting boards cut down to size. A circular saw is the perfect tool for the job. Here's why:

Price—A *good* circular saw sells for under $100, which is a fraction of what you would pay for other power saws that do the same kind of work. Someday you might want to buy a miter saw ($200+) or table saw ($500+), but for now, a circular saw will handle almost any job you can give it.

Easy to use—Circular saws are ready to go the minute you take them out of the box. Plus, the newer designs are small, lightweight, and less intimidating than older models.

OOPS!

Top 3 Mistakes Using a Circular Saw

Too Low!

Pinched Blade

I know it's tempting to cut a board on whatever is handy (chairs, tables, garbage cans). Precarious setups are sure to make your boards bow in the middle and pinch the blade, causing your saw to unexpectedly jump away from the cut.

Always make sure your work piece is securely *clamped on both sides* of the cut line. A simple pair of sawhorses make a perfect worktable for doing just that.

Blade Set Too Low

Some DIY newbies mistakenly set the blade at maximum depth so it will cut through any size board. That might be okay for 2x4s, but with thinner material it could be a problem—causing chipped edges, or worse, jerk the saw away from the board.

Keep your blade depth adjusted so you see only about ¼" of the blade through the underside of the board. This is especially important for smooth cuts in plywood.

Battery Left In

It's easy to remember to unplug corded tools before removing the blade—the cord is always there to remind us. Not so easy with cordless tools. It's easy to forget the power is always on—as long the battery is connected. This can be dangerous.

Get in the habit of always removing the battery before changing blades or messing with any of the adjustments. Play it safe with all cordless tools!

What You CAN Do with a Circular Saw...

Crosscuts

Just as the name implies, a crosscut goes *across* the width of a board, which effectively shortens the length. The best way to make crosscuts is with a straight edge guide, like the carpenter's square you see above. Be sure to clamp everything down and keep both hands on the saw. See page 40 for more details.

Rip Cuts

Ripping means making a long cut along the *length* of a board—which effectively reduces the width of that board. You'll need some type of ripping guide to get a clean, straight edge—either a metal guide from a woodworking supply store, or a cutting guide you make yourself. See page 41 for more details.

Plywood Cuts

A circular saw is a great tool for cutting down large plywood panels. One easy way to cut panels is to put a large sheet of Styrofoam on the floor, lay the plywood directly on top, and make the cut. Another option is to let your local home center of lumber store cut the panels for you. See page 127 for more details.

...And What You CAN'T

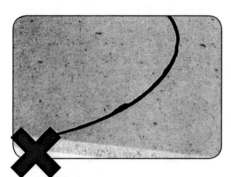

Cut Curves

Circular saws are made to cut straight lines and not much else, really. If you try cutting curves, you'll find your saw getting pinched and bound up in the wood.

Complex Joinery

Some people might attempt to use a circular saw to make complex joinery (like half laps), although I've found it best to leave this type of work for a table saw.

Must-Have Blades

Combination Blade
With 24 teeth, this fast-cutting blade is perfect for 2x4s and decking. The drawback? It leaves a fairly rough edge on a board.

Plywood Blade
With 100 teeth, this slow-cutting blade leaves a smooth edge on plywood, hardboard, and other thin laminates.

It's All in the Teeth

As a general rule, the more teeth on a blade, the smoother the cut. For example, a blade with 24 teeth (per inch) leaves a fairly rough edge, but is perfectly suited for building a deck or a shed. A blade with 100 teeth leaves a dramatically smoother edge, which makes it a better choice for cutting more fragile materials like plywood, hardboard, and laminates. Keep in mind that more teeth means a slower cutting speed.

Most Important Blade Adjustments

Blade Depth
Set the blade depth just deep enough to cut through the underside of the board—and no more. I like to see about ¼" of the blade peeking through the cut. This keeps everything smooth and clean—as well as preventing dangerous kickback from the blade.

You'll find the blade height knob located at the back of the saw.

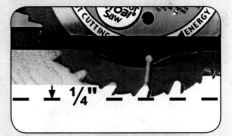

Set the blade to extend about ¼" through the board—but no more.

Blade Bevel
The tricky part about cutting a bevel is *accuracy*. Most saws come with an adjustment gauge mounted to the body, but it's a rough adjustment only. I like to make a few test cuts in scrap wood first, and then check the accuracy of the bevel with some other tool, like a protractor or a high-quality bevel gauge.

Look for the bevel knob located at the front of the saw.

Keep in mind that changing the bevel changes the cutting depth.

Changing Blades

The good news about changing circular saw blades is that you have only a couple parts that can get lost! The entire assembly consists of (1) a small screw that keeps the blade from coming off and (2) a washer on each side of the blade.

Can it Go On Backwards?

Unfortunately, yes. That's why you'll need to pay attention to where the blade teeth are pointing (up and towards the front). Or—just make sure the *printed* side of the blade is facing outward.

Remove Battery

After finding a flat, clean surface on which to work, first and foremost *remove the battery*. You might question the need to take this extra step—especially since the trigger switch has a safety lock in place. My opinion is that small, plastic parts (like the safety switch) are never fail-safe, and I'd rather not take the risk of losing a finger!

Lock Down Blade

Anyone new to changing saw blades will quickly discover that turning the wrench also turns the blade. More recent saws now include a small button (located behind the guard) that temporarily locks the blade in place—allowing you to easily remove the screw.

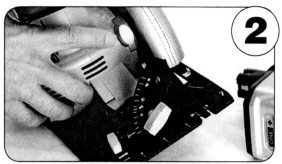

Remove Blade Screw

Don't be fooled by the "reverse-thread" screw. It simply means you'll need to turn the screw *right* to loosen, *left* to tighten. Once the blade screw is out, remove the outer washer and slip the blade out and away from the blade guard.

Replace Blade

Be sure to put the new blade on the same way the old blade came off—with the teeth pointing forward and the printed side of the blade facing outwards. You might also see arrows on the blade telling you in which direction the blade should spin after it's turned on (clockwise).

Corded vs Cordless...What's the Difference?

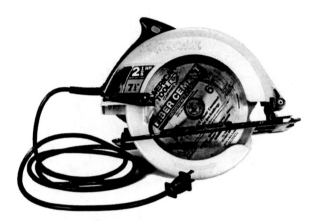

Corded

I have an old 7¼" Craftsman circular saw with a long cord sitting somewhere in my basement. The fact is, I rarely need that much power for the projects I build, so it doesn't get much use. However, for those down-and-dirty jobs that demand a little more muscle than my cordless can deliver, my old Craftsman is worth its weight in gold. Here's why.

Pros

If you're low on cash, an old-style circular saw with a cord can be bought cheap. In fact, you can probably find one at a neighborhood garage sale for just a few dollars. The fact is, an old circular saw like this will cut through wood as well as a cordless model—but with more brute strength. So I still find myself occasionally pulling out my tried-and-true Craftsman for the most demanding and dirty cutting jobs I come across. And don't forget that using a corded circular saw means you don't have to worry about keeping batteries charged. As long as you can find an outlet or a power strip, your corded circular saw is always ready to go.

Cons

For some reason a big circular saw with a cord never feels very good in my hands. It feels like it's made for someone else who works outside all day framing houses and building decks. It's heavy, loud, and tears through wood with what seems to be enough force to slice through concrete. It definitely gets the job done—it's just not very pleasant to use.

Cordless

Today you'll find that most of the circular saws in home centers are cordless—and for good reason. They're small, lightweight, and so easy to use that anyone with the notion to build something can get started in the craft. But that doesn't mean cordless circular saws are without fault. As tempting as it is to use them for every job that comes along, they do have their limits.

Pros

The best part about using a cordless circular saw is the *way it feels*. The compact design and reduced weight is a nice diversion from the older circular saws that tend to be larger and heavier. Although my Ryobi cordless (see photo above) has a 5½" blade—which is quite a bit smaller than the conventional 7¼" blade on my old Craftsman—it still cuts though through dimensional lumber (1x boards and 2x boards) with ease. My cordless Ryobi is lighter, more compact, and quieter than any of the corded tools I have in my shop. I also like the freedom it gives me not having to constantly struggle with a tangled cord.

Cons

Cordless circular saws tend to be a little more expensive than conventional saws that run on 120v. I've also discovered that replacing batteries (after a couple years) definitely adds more to the total investment. You'll also spend some extra cash if you want a cordless model designed for professional work—like framing houses and building decks.

Cordless Tool Batteries

Lithium-Ion

All of my Ryobi cordless tools use lithium-ion batteries. Most cordless tool manufacturers are switching over (if they haven't already), replacing the older nickel-cadmium style. So what's so special about lithium-ion? Check out the pros and cons below.

Lithium-Ion Batteries

Pros

Light Weight. At first you won't notice much difference in weight between a lithium battery and a nickel-cadmium battery. They're fairly close. But after a few hours of work, you'll definitely notice the difference—which means less muscle fatigue, which means more work gets done.

Long Charge. A lithium-ion battery holds a charge four times longer than a typical nickel-cadmium battery. That means for most jobs, you can get by with a single battery charger and one extra battery. Best part is you don't have to wait till the battery is completely dead before recharging (like the old nickel-cadmium).

Cons

Short Life Span. Lithium-Ion batteries aren't perfect. For example, they don't last forever. Most lithium-ion batteries will start failing after two or three years—regardless of how often you use them. So use them up now, and be ready to buy replacements later.

Sensitivity to Temperature. Lithium-ion batteries tend to be more sensitive to heat than nickel-cadmium, which can further reduce their already limited lifespan. For demanding jobs, like drilling holes in concrete, consider using a corded tool instead. Also, keep your batteries and charger in a cool place.

Speed

Torque Clutch

Chuck

Bit

Trigger

Rechargeable Battery

RYOBI

Lithium 18V

the powerhouse package
Drill & Driver

Cordless drill/drivers pack a punch in both power and features. The best part is that prices are lower than ever for great-quality brands and models.

Know these Controls

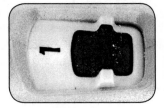

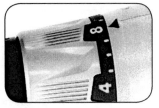

Trigger
A variable-speed trigger switch makes drilling easy. Above that is a forward/reverse switch, which you can easily reach with your thumb.

Speed
Most drills include two speed choices—one for drilling and one for driving screws. Believe it or not, this can make a big difference. See page 12.

Torque
Sometimes you need to curb the amount of power you unleash on a screw—to prevent stripping or driving screws too far into wood. See page 14.

Why a Cordless Drill?

It's funny that most of what I do with a drill has nothing to do with drilling. More often I'm driving screws, not making holes. Both are very different kinds of tasks, which explains why drills have so many knobs and adjustments. Hopefully these controls will make some sense as your read further.

A Note About Safety

When I talk about the dangers of using tools, it's hard to put the cordless drill in the same category as a tool like a circular saw, which can easily severe a hand or finger. However, that doesn't mean a cordless drill is harmless. An 18v motor has enough muscle to twist your elbow out of joint if you're not careful. The most likely time for this to happen is when the bit breaks through the backside of a board—which can cause the bit to bind up in the wood.

There's not much you can do to prevent this. Just be prepared with some extra gripping power as your bit breaks through to the other side of the board.

OOPS!

Top 3 Mistakes Using a Drill / Driver

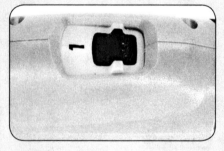

Wrong Speed

When switching between drill bits and drill drivers, most people forget to change the drill speed accordingly.

Use low-speed (1) for driving screws and bolts. This offers more control and more torque for driving stubborn woodscrews.

Use high speed (2) for drilling holes. This helps clear out sticky wood debris from the pilot hole while you drill.

Overworking

Cordless drills work fine for driving screws in bookcases and tables. However, be careful with larger projects.

Building a deck or shed can quickly overheat smaller cordless drills, shortening the life of the battery and the tool.

For the big jobs, consider using an *impact driver* to fasten hardware like lag screws and carriage bolts.

Using Dull Bits

We're all guilty—using the same bit over and over until we're doing nothing but stirring up a lot of heat

Dull bits not only waste time—they wear out the motor. When buying cheap bits, accept the fact that these are "disposable" bits.

That's why I like to keep a set of cheap bits for down-and-dirty jobs, and reserve my better-quality bits for wood projects.

What You CAN Do with a Cordless Drill...

Drill Pilot Holes

This is an easy task for cordless drills. The variable speed feature makes it easy to start the hole in the right location, but there are some other adjustments to consider too, particularly the speed setting.

Set Speed to High (2) for drilling holes. Pilot holes tend to get clogged up with pulp. The faster the bit speed, the better your drill can remove waste from the hole.

Drive Screws

I can't imagine building a wood project without using a power screwdriver. There are just too many fasteners in a typical project to do it any other way. Use the adjustable torque setting (page 14) for best results.

Set Speed to Low (1) for driving screws and fasteners. The slower speed allows more control and more torque for twisting stubborn woodscrews into place.

Cut Small Holes

A cordless drill works great for making small holes in wood. You'll find lots of hole-cutting accessories at your local home center. Most are designed for installing door locks, but you can use them for other things too.

Note: Don't overwork your drill by trying to cut holes more than a couple inches deep or a couple inches in diameter. These jobs are better suited for a jigsaw or drill press.

...And What You CAN'T

The Bigger Jobs

Everything has its limits. Jobs like cutting large circles, tightening carriage bolts, and boring deep holes might be better suited for a heavy-duty driver, or a ½" chuck drill with a cord.

Torque Adjustment

One of the most misunderstood features in a cordless drill/driver is the *torque adjustment*. This control lets you decide how much raw power the driver will unleash on a screw or fastener.

That's important because an 18-volt motor carries a fairly big punch, which makes it easy to strip the head of a screw, or drive the screw so far into a board that it comes out the other side (yikes).

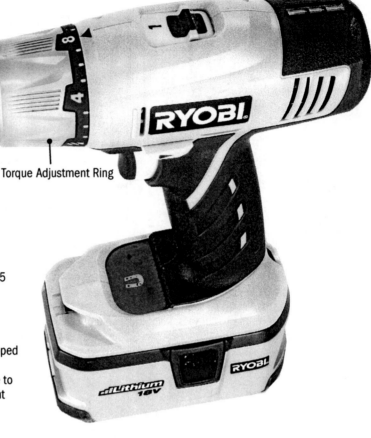

Chuck

Torque Adjustment Ring

That's where the torque adjustment on your drill/driver comes to the rescue. Look for an adjustable ring located behind the chuck that starts at 0 and goes up to 20 or 25 (depending on the model). Zero is the softest setting—while 25 unleashes the full power of the tool on a fastener.

The best way to find the ideal torque setting for driving a particular screw is to start out at zero and slowly move up in numbers. A loud "clacking" sound means your driver has stopped turning the screw. Keep adding more torque until the screw rests just below the surface of the board—but no farther. I like to experiment on a scrap piece of wood first, finding just the right setting for the project at hand.

GOOD

BETTER

BEST

Steel
Cheap & Easy

Black Oxide
Heat Resistant

Titanium
Toughest Bit

drilling holes with
Twist Bits

It's easy to be overwhelmed by the number of different bits you'll find at a home center. However, for most small projects, the selection can be narrowed down to just a few choices—bits that will handle almost any job you'll face in the shop (see below).

Why So Many Colors?
Color indicates the type of coating applied to the bit at the factory. The primary purpose of a coating is to reduce heat—an important feature for drilling holes in steel, but not so much for drilling in wood.

The Only Bits You Really Need

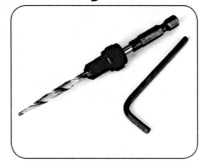

Pilot-Point

Look for twist bits with a *pilot-point*—a feature that makes starting pilot holes in wood *much* easier (and more accurate) than other bits.

Combination

This bit features a tapered shaft and countersink head, designed to better accommodate the shape of a typical woodscrew (see page 82).

Self-Centering

This bit is a must-have item for installing hinges. The clever tool keeps your pilot hole perfectly centered in each hole of the hinge.

Page 82 Learn More About:
Drilling Pilot Holes

driving screws with
Driver Bits

Sometimes I get overwhelmed with all the drivers and attachments I see at hardware stores and home centers. Trying to decide which items to buy can be a challenge. I've found that for most small projects, the three basic drivers listed below are all you really need to get the job done.

The Only Drivers You Really Need

Phillips Head

Since a *Phillips woodscrew* is one of the most common screws around, you'll need a *Phillips driver*—and plenty of them (they get lost easily). I like to keep several different sizes in the shop, including the extra-long sizes for getting my driver into narrow spaces.

Square Head

You'll find square heads in pocket hole screws, drywall screws, and a few other fasteners. That's enough reason to keep at least a couple *square head* drivers in your shop. Note: Most pocket hole *kits* include a square head driver bit in the package.

Nut Driver

Some projects call for heavy-duty fasteners—like lag screws or carriage bolts. You can use a socket wrench to drive the screws manually, but a nut driver attached to your cordless drill makes the job of driving large fasteners quick and easy.

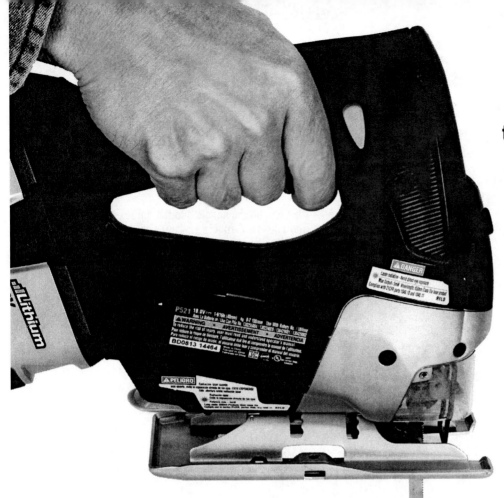

tricky twists & turns
Jig Saw

At a fraction of the cost of more expensive scroll saws, a jigsaw is the perfect tool for making tricky cuts in your next wood project.

Know these Controls

  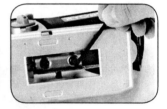

Trigger

Like the circular saw, a jigsaw includes a safety-lock that keeps you from accidentally starting the blade when picking up the tool.

Orbit

Orbit controls the cutting pattern of the blade, which can be adjusted to better match the material you are using. See page 21.

Bevel

Probably not something you'll use very often, but nice to have when you need it. Use an angle gauge tool for setting precise bevel cuts.

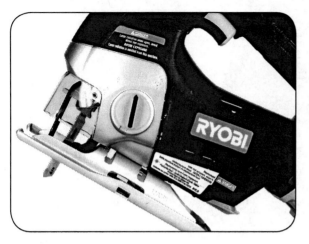

Why a Jigsaw?

When it comes to cutting curves in wood, the jigsaw is hard to beat for its low cost and simple operation. You'll spend only fraction of what you would pay for its closest cousins— the scroll saw and the band saw—and it's so easy to use that you might even forget that you're using a saw (safety warning: a jigsaw can cut fingers like any other power saw).

With a nice, tight grip on the handle and the proper set up (boards secured and clamped to a sawhorse or bench), a jigsaw can be one of the most versatile and fun tools to have in your shop.

OOPS!

Top 3 Mistakes Using a Jigsaw

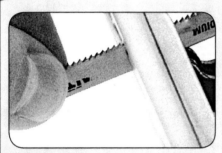

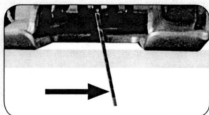

Wrong Blade

A jigsaw works well only if you have the right blade installed for the material you are cutting. The wrong blade will bring the motor down to a slow and battery-draining grind. Take the time to switch blades when switching between different materials.

Pushing

It's easy to get impatient with a jigsaw and try to speed up the cut by pushing the saw forward. However, forward pressure can make the blade bend—creating a small bevel to the cut. Worse yet, it can also cause a blade to snap.

Pinching

If the material you are cutting is not properly supported, the weight of the saw can make it sag in the middle and collapse against the blade. This will make the saw stop, stray off path, or worse, jump dangerously up and away from the surface.

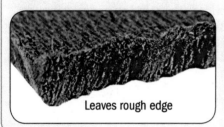

Leaves rough edge

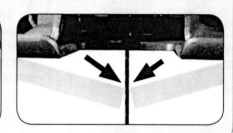

What You CAN Do With a Jig Saw...

Cut Circles

Cutting circles in wood is a task that not many tools can do. A jigsaw makes the job surprisingly quick and easy. I like to start by drilling a large pilot hole near the edge of the circle (a). Then I simply lower the jigsaw blade into the hole (b) and start cutting along the circular path.

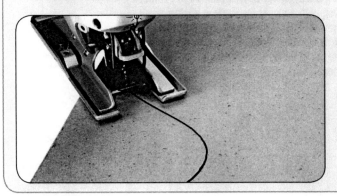

Cut Curves

I think what I like most about a jigsaw is how well it handles intricate and complicated curves—the kind of curves that are normally made on expensive shop tools like band saws and scroll saws. A jigsaw is also perfect for cutting small notches, indents, dips, angles, decorative edges, and patterns—all for $75 or less.

...And What You CAN'T

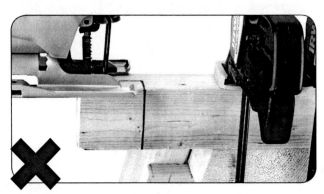

Complex Joinery

I've tried cutting joinery with a jigsaw—like half lap joints on outdoor construction projects—but I've never had much success with that. The blade doesn't seem stable enough to cut a square edge (shoulder) that you'll need for accurate joinery. I usually have better luck cutting joints like this with a hand saw.

Most jigsaws come with two blades—one for cutting wood, the other for metal. You'll likely need to buy more.

Metal Blade

Wood Blade

Jigsaw Blades

What's Included

My first jigsaw came with two blades. I used the first blade on everything until it broke—and then used the other blade until it was so dull it wouldn't cut paper. Since then I've learned a few things about jigsaw blades and how to use them. It all starts with the teeth.

It's the Teeth

At first glance, jigsaw blades all look the same. However, with a closer inspection, you'll see it's the *teeth* that set them apart. Some blades have hundreds of small teeth, while other blades have fewer teeth more widely spaced. In general, the more teeth on a blade, the smoother the cut.

The Blades You Really Need

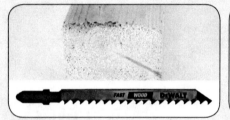

Rough Wood Blade

With less than 10 teeth per inch, this blade is perfect for quick cuts in thick boards like 2x4s and wood posts.

Smooth Wood Blade

With twice as many teeth, this blade leaves a nice, smooth edge on 1x pine, MDF, and particle board.

Laminate Blade

I like to use a laminate blade for getting a super-smooth edge on thin plywood, hardboard, and plastics.

Choosing The Right Shank

The shank is the part of the blade that fits into the saw—with a small notch or hole that locks the blade in place. Some blades have a **T-Shank** while other blades have a **Universal shank**. Some jigsaws accept both styles—but some do not. Be sure to check your jigsaw owner's manual to find out which style of shank your particular saw requires.

T-Shank   **Universal Shank**

Changing Blades

My Ryobi has a spring-loaded clamp that lets me change blades using my thumb. Other saws might require a hex-head wrench.

Other Features on a Jigsaw

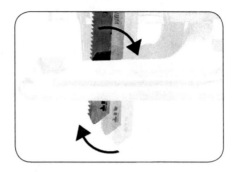
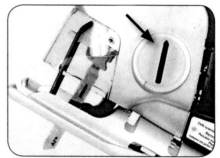

Orbital Action

A good-quality jigsaw will usually feature *orbital action*—a circular up-and-down path that forces the blade to cut on the *upstroke only*. Orbital action can make your saw cut more aggressively, which means a faster cut through wood. Plus, it reduces the amount of wear and tear on the blade (the teeth don't touch the board on the down stroke). Orbital action is fairly common with jigsaws in the $75 - $100 price range.

Most jigsaws with orbital motion let you control *how much* orbital action to apply. For example, if I need to make some quick cuts through thick pine, I'll use full-strength orbital action and run the motor as fast as it will go.

Faster isn't always better, though. With more dense material (like plastic), those same settings would probably melt the material (from too much heat), and/or break the blade. For non-wood materials like plastic, metal, and hardboard, set your jigsaw to run at a slower speed with no orbital action.

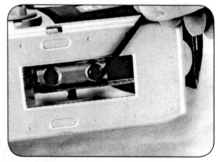

Bevel Cuts

Jigsaws can cut a fairly decent bevel, although I've found the mechanism for making this adjustment to be awkward and inaccurate. On most saws, you'll make the adjustment by pivoting the base of the saw itself, which then changes the cutting angle of the blade. Some jigsaws include a bevel guide, but don't assume this is even close to being accurate. The only way to get your jigsaw to cut a true, accurate bevel is by trial and error.

Always make a few test cuts using a piece of scrap wood and a *real* bevel gauge—checking the angle of the cut after each test run. Once you have the correct bevel on your test board, tighten the bevel adjustment on the saw and move on to the real work piece.

Although the bevel feature might be helpful for creating certain types of project joinery, the more popular application is in scrolling and decorative work—where a small bevel on the cut line gives an interesting look and feel to the overall project.

how to build anything
3 Boards
Inexpensive dimensional lumber is perfect for making simple projects.

2x Lumber

1x Lumber

Plywood

Nominal	Actual
2x4	1½ x 3½
2x6	1½ x 5½
2x8	1½ x 7¼
2x10	1½ x 9¼
2x12	1½ x 11¼

2x6

2x4

Nominal vs Actual
When designing a project, keep in mind that the actual dimensions of a board are somewhat smaller than what you see on the label (nominal dimensions).

Board Length
Another label you might find confusing on 2x lumber is the board length. Some 2x boards are cut to 96" (8 ft.)—while others curiously measure 92 5/8" long. The difference won't mean much to us building a workbench or a shelf, but for a carpenter putting up a wall in a house, 92 5/8" is the exact size needed to fit a board between the bottom and top plates of an typical 8' wall. Look to see if your store has a special discount on "studs"—which they often do.

2x Lumber

Sometimes called "sticks" or "studs" by contractors, 2x lumber (pronounced "two-by") is cheap, strong, and perfect for building simple wood projects. Most 2x lumber you'll find at a home center comes from either spruce, pine, or fir trees, depending on which type of wood the supplier has at the time. Not that this makes any difference to us really, all three species are very similar. It does, however, explain the mysterious "SPF" label: **S=Spruce, P=Pine, F=Fir.**

2x4—Sometimes called "sticks" or "studs," 2x4s are nearly indestructible.

2x6—Great for the roof of your house—and for smaller projects, too.

Projects You Can Build with 2x Lumber

Workbenches—2x lumber is perfect for building benches, worktables, and other furniture for the shop.

Sawhorses—2x4s are the ideal boards for making a super-strong sawhorse for cutting and assembling projects.

Sheds & Playhouses—2x lumber works just as well for building a shed as it does for building a house.

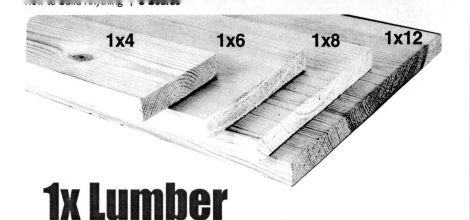

1x4   1x6   1x8   1x12

Nominal	Actual
1x4	³⁄₄ x 3½
1x6	³⁄₄ x 5½
1x8	³⁄₄ x 7¼
1x10	³⁄₄ x 9¼
1x12	³⁄₄ x 11¼

Nominal vs Actual

When designing a wood project, keep in mind that the actual dimensions of the board are somewhat smaller than what's printed on the label and signs displayed in the store (nominal). See chart above.

1x Lumber

Another inexpensive type of wood that works great for building simple projects is 1x pine (pronounced "one-by"). Most stores carry 1x pine boards in two different grades—"common" and "select." It's easy to spot the difference—*common* boards are riddled with knots and holes, while *select* boards are clean and free of defects. Expect to pay 3-4 times the price for select-grade boards, though.

Most for Your Money

The challenge for budget-minded project builders is to carefully sort through the common-grade lumber and find boards with the *fewest number of defects*. You might be surprised just how clean of a board you can find in the common-grade lumber bins.

Spend More for Quality

If common-grade boards seem too rough, consider a more expensive grade called "select" —usually available in both pine and poplar. The boards are extremely clean and smooth, and have none of the knots or defects found in common grade boards. Some are even wrapped in plastic. Be careful though—these boards will cost you three times the price of common-grade lumber.

Board Grades

Common—knots & holes, but less expensive.

Select—clear and smooth, but at a price.

Projects You Can Build with 1x Lumber

Cabinet Frames—1x lumber is perfect for building the inner frame (carcass) of a large box or cabinet (page 63).

Shelving—1x lumber is ideal for building shelves and storage units located around the house and shop.

Bookcases—1x12s provide just enough shelf depth (11 ¼") to make a solid-wood bookcase for the home.

Buying Lumber—What to Avoid

Cup

Boards with *cup* have a "U" shape from edge to edge—making them useless for building anything. The best way to check for cup is to lay the board flat and look for a side-to-side rocking motion. Be sure to flip the board over and check the other side, too.

Sometimes you'll find the lumber bins at a home center are riddled with boards that are warped and twisted. Not a big problem if you're building a house or garage (there are work arounds for this), but for smaller projects, you'll need to be careful to avoid boards that have **cup, bow, or twist**.

Bow

Bow is easy to spot. Hold the board edge-side up and peer down the full length with one eye. This will quickly tell you if the piece is warped from one end to the other. If you plan to cut the board in smaller pieces, a certain amount of bow won't hurt. However, if you need the full length—for projects like a workbench or picnic table, set the board aside and keep looking.

Crook

Unfortunately a board with zero cup and zero bow can *still be crooked*. Best way to spot crook is to hold the board surface-side up and peer down the full length of the board. A severe case of crook makes an otherwise straight board look like a road with a curve. Unless you plan to cut this board into a lot of smaller pieces, set this aside and keep looking.

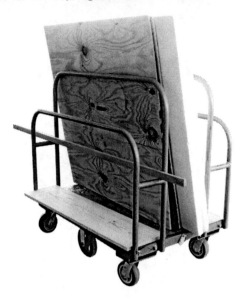

Pulling Boards

Employees at most home centers *usually* understand that project builders need to sort through the lumber stacks to find usable boards. If you do it the right way (see box at right), you'll avoid making enemies at the store. You'll also avoid hurting yourself in the process—which is easy to do when digging through lumber!

THINK SAFETY

Wear Gloves!
Gloves will protect you from nasty splinters and jagged edges—plus all the other sharp and pointy edges lurking throughout a typical store.

Keep Bar Codes Together
There's no reason to make checkout clerks search for bar codes. When back in the lumber aisle, arrange the boards on the cart so all the stickers are showing at one end.

Sort with Two Carts

Keep Cart

Most people attempt to sort lumber by pulling bad boards to the front of the pile or pushing them to the back. This leaves an unstable (and dangerous) gutter in the center of the stack. This method also makes it difficult for the next shopper to find any usable lumber, which is now covered and trapped under the rubble.

Reject Cart

A better approach to sorting lumber is to use *two lumber carts*—one cart for stacking boards you want to keep—and another cart for rejects. Once you have the boards you want, be sure to put the discards back on the shelf—but away from the main stack. Or ask a store employee where he/she prefers to locate defective boards.

That's a Good Question!

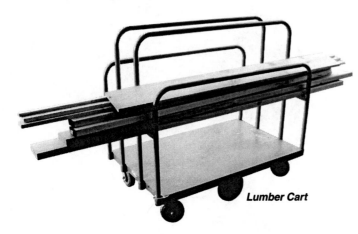
Shopping Cart

Q. Can I use a shopping cart?

A. I won't say *never* use a grocery-style cart to take wood to the checkout aisle. Sometimes carts are just easier to maneuver through narrow aisles, especially when I have only a couple small boards to buy. The operative word here is *small*. Large boards tend to slide around on plastic carts, making the trip to the checkout aisle too precarious. Better to start things off right by snatching up one of the metal lumber carts from the board aisle. They're perfect for moving both boards and large sheets of plywood all in one trip to the front of the store. You can also toss your other project supplies on for the ride.

Q. Will they cut boards for me?

A. This might depend on the particular store, but as a general rule, home centers and lumber stores will cut boards down to size for you—*at no charge*. This can make the task of getting large pieces (like plywood) to your home a whole lot easier, especially if you don't have a truck. Keep in mind that most stores have a limit to how much free cutting they will do for you. It's usually around three or four cuts maximum. If you need more, the store might quote you a price—somewhere around 50 cents per cut. That's well worth the money.

Shopping Cart vs Lumber Cart
Shopping carts are okay for moving a few small boards, but use lumber carts for moving a large project.

Q. Do I need a Truck?

A. Of course the easiest way to get lumber home is with a truck. If you don't have your own, consider either renting a truck from the home center, or have the materials delivered. You can usually do either for less than $50 —and not have to worry about ripping up upholstery or putting dents in your own car.

For smaller wood projects, a car or van should work fine. I spent many years hauling lumber and supplies in a small hatchback. I've also loaded lumber in a sedan by removing the back seat and shoving 2x4s through the trunk, with the ends of the boards resting on the front dash. It's a little rough on the upholstery, but it gets the job done.

Lumber Cart

Cut Lumber Before You Bring it Home
A little known secret about home centers is that most will cut your lumber for free. If not, the low prices they charge for cutting is still a bargain.

Use the Rental Truck
Most home centers have a truck available for rent, which is always cheaper than repairing the damage you might do to your car.

Plywood

Plywood makes it possible to cover large areas of a project without spending a fortune on wood to do it.

Why So Many Kinds of Plywood?

If you've ever wandered around the lumber section at your local home improvement center, you've seen the endless stacks of plywood lined up and down the aisles. The variety can be overwhelming, with cryptic labels that most store employees don't understand. Some plywood panels can cost as little as $10, and others nearly $100. So how do you decide which plywood to buy for a project? Let's start at the beginning, and try to clear up some of the confusion in what makes one plywood panel different from another.

Construction plywood   Project plywood

Construction Plywood vs Project Plywood

First understand that home improvement centers cater not only to homeowners, but also to general contractors. That means *a lot* of the plywood you see in the aisles at a "big box" store is made for *construction*—roofing houses, building garages, and covering bathroom floors (actually it's called sheathing). The kind of plywood better suited for building wood *projects*—like cabinets and furniture— is located a little deeper in the aisles.

This doesn't mean you *can't* use construction plywood for small projects. In fact, plywood sheathing might be a good economical choice for things like shelving in the garage, storage cabinets in the basement—or anything where function is more important than appearance. Sheathing might be a little rough to the touch, but it's an amazingly strong and durable piece of material. Best part is the price—which is well below the cost of other types of plywood.

Know your Plywood

OSB—Inexpensive construction sheathing best suited for "roughing in" outdoor projects like sheds and playhouses. Often called *chipboard* panels.

CDX—Another type of construction sheathing that *might* work okay for rough shop projects, like work tables and storage. It's moisture resistant.

Sanded Pine—With its clean, smooth surface (one or both sides), sanded pine is perfect for building boxes, cabinets, and fine furniture.

Baltic Birch—Here's the ultimate plywood for building nice shop furniture. No need to hide the edges, the multiple veneer layers add beauty to the project!

Plywood Letter Grades

What do the Letters Mean?

Plywood uses a universal coding system where the first letter refers to the quality of veneer on the *front* of the panel, and the second letter refers to the veneer on the *back*. Some types of plywood include a third letter (X), which refers to the type of glue used in production (see outdoor plywood page 30).

Best quality veneer available. Might include a few small knots or defects that have been patched. Sanded smooth. Good choice for projects like cabinets and furniture.

A few more surface defects than what you'll find in A. Also sanded smooth and ready for finishing. Good choice for simple wood projects around the home.

Large knots up to 1½" diameter, as well as small holes, defects, and some discoloration. Not sanded. Good choice for rough construction projects like sheds and playhouses.

Lowest quality veneer you can buy. Includes large and small knots, splits, and defects that are not repaired. Not sanded. Mostly used for very rough construction work.

Type of glue used to bond the veneers. The letter "X" stands for "exposure" (not exterior), which means it must eventually be covered by another material (like shingles).

Indoor   Outdoor (pressure treated)

Indoor vs Outdoor

Where you plan to locate the finished project—in the house or in the backyard—makes a big difference in the kind of plywood you should buy. Plywood manufacturers are very specific about this difference, and are careful to label their products for indoor or outdoor use.

Plywood for Indoor Projects

For projects that never see the light of day (like cabinets and shop furniture) you'll find a wide range of plywoods to choose from. Whether your local home center has all of them in stock is another matter, but most stores will have the types I've listed below.

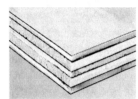

Pine Veneer Plywood

Pine Veneer

Usually labeled "Sanded Pine BC" or "Sandeply," these panels work great for wood projects. The 4x8 sheets are inexpensive ($20 or less) with one side sanded smooth for painting or finishing.

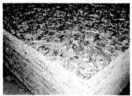

OSB "Chip Board"

Oriented Strand Board (OSB)

Sometimes called "chip board," OSB is made from wood chips glued together in an odd, patchwork design. The crude surface might be too rough for some projects, but that's a judgement call you can make for yourself.

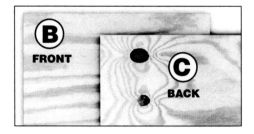

Good Side—Bad Side

Most plywood is manufactured so that one side has a better grade veneer than the other (see grading system above). This makes good economic sense since one side of a panel will not likely be seen in the finished project (cabinets and enclosed boxes).

Plywood for Outdoor Projects

Weather is hard on any kind of wood, but it's especially hard on the delicate wood veneers in a sheet of plywood. Rain, sleet, snow, and even the sun itself can quickly destroy plywood in just a few months. And that's not including damage from insects. The only practical solution for using plywood outdoors is to buy plywood that's made especially *for the outdoors*. However, be careful not to confuse the words "outdoor," "exterior," and "pressure treated" to all mean the same thing. In many cases, they don't. Some types of outdoor plywood can withstand years of direct exposure to rain and snow, some can't.

Pressure-Treated

Pressure-Treated Plywood

Saturated with chemicals to ward off mold, mildew, and insects, pressure-treated plywood can survive outside for decades without paint or a protective finish. In most home centers, pressure-treated lumber is located in its own aisle, and has a distinctive green cast.

CDX Sheathing

CDX Sheathing

CDX sheathing is used mostly by contractors for exterior walls and roofs. The letters "CD" represent the veneer grades used on the front and back (see letter codes on page 29). "X" refers to glue (not the wood) and means the material is rated for outdoor *exposure* (eventually the panel must be covered by something more weather resistant—like siding or shingles).

CDX can be an inexpensive alternative to more expensive plywood, although it's considerably more rough on both the surface and the edges. For down-and-dirty projects, like garage shelves and storage bins, CDX can be a good choice for the budget-minded.

CDX Roofing & Siding

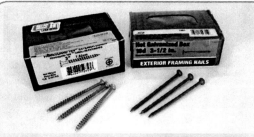

Exterior-Grade Fasteners

The chemicals in pressure-treated plywood will corrode and destroy metals—up to five times faster than untreated wood. That means for outdoor projects, you'll need to use special hardware and fasteners. Look for boxes labeled *exterior*, *galvanized*, or *stainless steel*.

Work Safely!

Inhaling dust from any type of wood can be dangerous, but dust from *treated* lumber can be especially toxic. Always wear a good dust mask and clear goggles when cutting treated lumber. If possible, try to work with treated lumber outside and away from your house.

Also, some consumer advocate groups are concerned about the possible health hazards of adhesive chemicals used in plywood—especially urea formaldehyde and phenol formaldehyde. As a result, some plywood manufacturers now use low formaldehyde-emitting glue systems, denoted by an "E" rating. Check with your local plywood supplier and ask about E-rated plywood.

Storing Plywood in the Shop

It's amazing how fast plywood can warp, especially when leaning against a wall (like most of us do with plywood when we get it home!). The best way store plywood is to keep the panels as upright as possible, and off the floor (to prevent panels from soaking up moisture in concrete).

To accomplish this, you can always build an elaborate storage system to hold the panels upright (like you might see in woodworking magazines). Or using a little ingenuity, take a look around in your shop and see what you already have at your disposal. For example, I like to use a couple extra hand clamps and a speed square to temporarily store my plywood panels.

Secure the Top
A simple hand clamp placed at the top of the panel keeps my plywood upright and away from the wall.

Secure the Bottom
An inexpensive speed square works great to keep my plywood panel from toppling over in the shop.

Buying Plywood

Once you've found the perfect plywood for your project, the next step is getting the wood out of the store and transported home (without anyone getting hurt!). The process can be more challenging than you think, considering the size and weight of a typical plywood panel. Here are few tricks I've learned along the way.

Moving Plywood Through the Store

For starters, be sure to snatch up one of the metal lumber carts *before* you start looking for plywood. Don't even think about using the plastic shopping carts—they're too small and flimsy for moving plywood. Lumber carts should be easy to find, somewhere near the 2x4s and 2x6s. The upright style (see photo at left) lets you stack plywood panels vertical, which makes them much easier to handle. However, if you have more than two or three panels to buy, use one of the flat metal carts instead, and stack the panels on top of each other.

Use the Contractor Checkout Counter

Sadly, I've actually seen people try to drag plywood through the main checkout aisles. Besides being awkward and difficult, this approach is dangerous to other customers. For everyone's sake, use the **contractor's checkout counter** when buying large items like plywood. If you have a lot of smaller items to buy on the same trip, consider buying and loading up your plywood first, then go back in with a plastic cart to finish up your shopping.

Getting Plywood Home

Store Delivery
Sometimes it makes more sense to have your plywood delivered, especially if you have a large project that includes other materials. Most stores charge around $50 to deliver materials to your house.

Rent a Truck
Most home centers rent pickups for around $20/hour. The only problem is timing—it's strictly a first-come, first-serve program. Best to avoid busy weekends and rent your truck during the week.

Use a Car?
There's really no good way to get plywood home in a car. Maybe you've heard the horror stories—like people loading plywood to a car roof or hanging it outside the door. Don't even try it.

Measuring & Marking Plywood

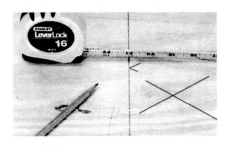

The Right Tools
Unfortunately, the tools I like to use for marking up 2x and 1x boards are pretty much useless for marking up a 4x8 sheet of plywood. Below I'll take a look at a few tricks I've discovered that make measuring and marking plywood easier, more efficient—and more accurate.

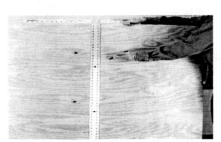

Use a Drywall Square
The *drywall square* has become one of my favorite tools in the shop for measuring and marking plywood panels. Essentially it's a 48" T-Square and ruler—which makes it a perfect companion to the 48" width of a plywood panel.

Best Tool For Cutting Plywood
A simple and inexpensive circular saw happens to be one of the best tools for cutting plywood. The panels are simply too big and awkward to maneuver on a table saw, and too large to cut with a radial arm saw or chop saw.

On the Floor with Styrofoam
Probably the easiest place to cut plywood is on a garage or basement floor. Of course you'll need some way to keep the blade from hitting concrete—and that's where Styrofoam comes in.

You can buy thick Styrofoam sheets in the building supplies section at your local home center. Ask them to cut a 4x8 sheet in half for you (this makes it a lot easier to get home). Lay the two sections on the floor, leaving a 4" gap in the middle. The gap allows space for clamping your cutting guide to the plywood (see photo left).

Page 127 Make Your Own:
Cutting Guide

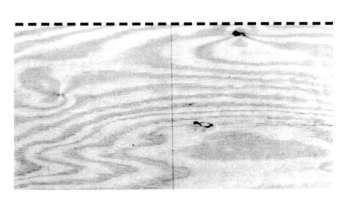

Use the Factory-Cut Edge?
Most woodworkers cringe at the idea of using a factory-cut edge on a project. Instead, they square up all sides of their lumber (with table saws and jointers) before they measure and layout their pieces. This can be an important step for furniture projects that need exact, unforgiving dimensions.

However, for simple wood projects made from 2x4s and plywood, the factory-cut edge may be as straight and square as you'll ever need it to be. Just be sure to use the factory edge as your starting point for all measurements. This will ensure that all sides of your project piece are square to each other.

Cutting Plywood

Get the Right Blade

Plywood is a somewhat fragile material that requires a little extra care when cutting. That includes using a saw blade that's specially designed for plywood. Most circular saws include a plywood blade in the package, or you can buy the blades at your local home center.

It's all in the Teeth

As a general rule, the more teeth on a blade, the smoother the cut. A *plywood blade* typically has **100 teeth** per inch, which helps prevent tearing along the edge of a cut. In contrast, a *combination blade* (general purpose blade) has only **24 teeth** per inch, which cuts fast but leaves a fairly rough edge.

Hiding Rough Plywood Edges

As careful as you might be to choose the right blade for the job, most types of plywood will still leave a relatively rough edge that you might want conceal. Or maybe you simply don't want the veneer stripes to show on the finished project. The easiest way to conceal a plywood edge is to attach decorative molding or self-adhesive veneer strips.

Decorative Molding

In the wood molding section at your local home center you'll find a wide variety of materials you can use to cover the rough edge of a plywood panel. With the right molding, you can completely hide all evidence that your project is even made from plywood.

Veneer Strips

Self-adhesive veneer strips do a nice job of concealing the edge of a plywood panel, especially hardwood plywood. The strips are sized to match the *actual* thickness of a 3/4" panel (which is 13/16"). Veneer strips can be found online or at woodworking supply stores.

Smoother Cuts in Plywood

Good side of plywood should face down when cutting with a circular saw.

Good Side Down

Saw blades tend to leave a smoother cut on one side of the board than the other. When using a circular saw to cut plywood, the cleanest side of the cut will be on the **underside** of the panel, not the top. Always place the good side of your panel **facing down** when cutting. *Note: When cutting plywood on a table saw, the opposite is true.*

Set blade so teeth cut just below the surface.

Set Blade Depth

One common cause of rough cuts in plywood is a blade set too low. This creates an overly sharp angle for the teeth as they bite into the wood. You can avoid the problem by setting the blade depth so teeth are cutting just below the surface of the board.

how to build anything
3 Steps

Break down the confusing process of construction into three simple steps.

Measure & Mark ......page 35

Clamp & Cut ....page 39

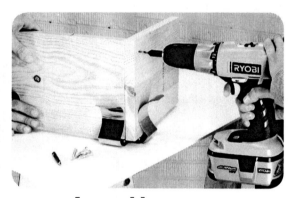

Assembly ....page 42

Tape Measure

Square

Compass

Measure & Mark

Tape Measure

One of the quickest and easiest ways to measure parts for a wood project is to use a measuring tape. Which brand you pick isn't that important. What *is* important is that you **use the same tape throughout the entire project** (tape measures are notoriously inconsistent from one brand to the next).

Tape Measure Tips & Tricks

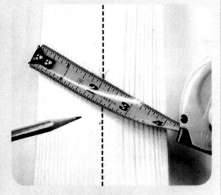

Loose Hook?

Of course it's the hook that makes a tape measure the handy tool that it is. But have you ever wondered why the hook is so loose and wobbly?

Note that the hook slides only as far as the thickness of the hook itself, which keeps the end of the tape perfectly "zeroed out" when pulling the tape (for outside measurements) or pushing the tape (for inside measurements).

Get Accurate

The concave surface of a tape measure tends to pull it away from the board you need to mark, making it difficult to get an accurate reading.

An easy solution is to simply twist the tape to one side while holding it against your work piece. The edge of the tape will quickly go flush against the surface of the board—letting you easily mark the location with super, pinpoint accuracy.

Quick Division

Another trick I like to use with a tape measure is finding the exact center of a board—without having to calculate the number in my head.

Simply catch the hook against one side and pull the tape at an angle across the width. Keep pulling until you can line up an even number on the opposite side. Divide that number in two to find the exact center of the board.

Combination Square

I normally avoid tools that are designed to do a lot of different things—because they usually don't do *any* of those things very well. Not so with this tool. Seems like no matter what job I start in the shop, the *combination square* is the first thing I grab to get a project started. As you'll see below, the tool makes common tasks extremely quick and easy.

Combination squares can cost anywhere from $10 to $100—depending on brand and quality. I've found the less expensive squares to work fine for most projects.

What You Can Do with a Combination Square

Mark Crosscuts

The 90-degree angle makes this square perfect for quickly marking crosscuts on a board. Push the handle up snug against the side of a board while you draw a pencil line across the width. This makes the process an easy two-hand operation.

Mark Rip Cuts

I used to draw rip lines by making a long series of checks along the edge of a board. My combination square changed all that. Now all I do is slide the square along the edge of the board—with my pencil following along in its path.

Copy & Transfer

Sometimes the best way to measure is to not measure at all. The combination square is the perfect tool for this. Just slide out the adjustable rule to match the width, length, or depth of a shape, and then transfer that measurement.

Compass

Sometimes a project calls for a series of holes or fasteners to be evenly spaced across a board. In most cases, it doesn't really make much difference what the *exact* distance is between the points, as long as they are *evenly* spaced. Sure, we could always grab a ruler and make a lot of complicated measurements to get everything where it should be, but a compass simplifies the task.

First extend the compass to match the distance you want between each point. Then "flip" the compass end-to-end, marking each point as you go.

Compass Tips & Tricks

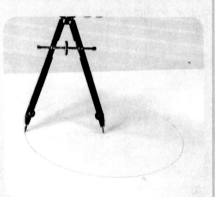

Pilot Holes

A compass makes quick and easy work of making sure all your nails and woodscrews are evenly spaced along the edge or the length of a board.

Copy & Transfer

A compass is a great tool for transferring exact dimensions from one thing to another—all without taking a lot of complicated measurements.

Draw Circles?

Okay, I saved the most obvious for last. Of course, a compass is perfect for drawing circles, rounded corners, and arcs on wood project pieces.

Avoid Measuring Mistakes

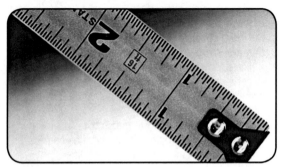

Measure as You Go

At first it might seem like a good idea to measure and cut all project pieces *before* you put them together. The problem is that regardless of how careful you measure, there will always be one piece that doesn't fit the space available. A better approach is to measure and cut boards *as you go*—making each project piece only after you have carefully measured the space it needs to fit.

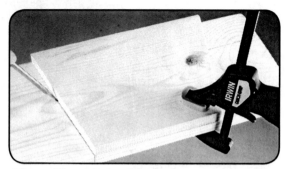

Use Templates

Most wood projects have several components that are identical in size and shape. You can always measure and mark each piece separately, but that's just asking for errors. Instead, use the first piece as a template for laying out and cutting the other pieces. You can make templates from almost anything that's easy to cut—like thin sheets of plywood or even cardboard.

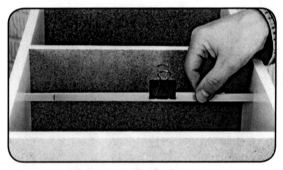

Use a Story Stick

A story stick is nothing more than simple device to mark dimensions without using a tape measure or ruler. Here I'm using two small pieces of wood (held together with an office paper clip) to find the inside dimension of a box, which could be difficult to measure otherwise.

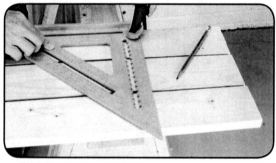

Gang Up Parts

One way to reduce chance of error in measuring is to mark up as many boards as possible *at the same time*. First group the project pieces together on a table and clamp everything down straight and square. Then draw the cut line across all pieces.

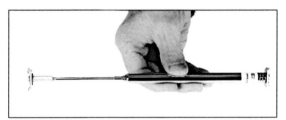

Why Measure?

This unique expandable rod lets you record exact dimensions from some of the most hard-to-measure spaces you can imagine—all without having to struggle with a tape or ruler. Then it's simply a matter of transferring that dimension to the board you want to cut.

www.ezwoodshop.com/ezstorystick.html

Clamp & Cut

These simple guidelines for cutting wood can make project building quick and easy—and more importantly, safe.

Irwin® Quick-Grip®
Most-used tool in my shop!

Cross-Cut or Rip-Cut?

Cross-Cuts ....page 40
Cross-cuts are made across the *width* of a board—to shorten the overall length.

Rip-Cuts ....page 41
Rip cuts are made along the *length* of a board—to reduce the overall width.

Cross Cuts

A circular saw is the perfect tool for cutting boards down to a specific *length* (*cross cut*). And when you gang up several boards together for the same cut (see tips below), you'll really start to see the advantages in using a circular saw.

Probably the best way to make cross cuts is with a guide or jig—and in an ideal world, with both hands on the saw while you cut. Of course this means clamping the board down on a sawhorse or a table before you start, a step that is often tempting to skip. Just remember that spending a few minutes beforehand to set up a proper workstation pays off in more ways than one. You'll not only get better results from your saw, but you'll also avoid serious accidents common with first-time builders.

Cross Cut Tips & Tricks

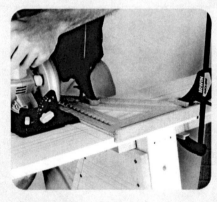

Quick Square

Plastic rafter squares (quick square) are perfect for making 90-degree cross cuts with a circular saw. It's an easy two-hand operation: one hand on the square, one hand on the saw. However, for most cuts, I like to clamp the square in place so I can have both hands on the saw.

Safe Stop

I know it's tempting to pull the saw up and away from the board immediately after cutting through lumber. Please leave that kind of Rambo-drama for Hollywood. Be safe and always let your saw blade come to a ***complete stop*** before moving the tool away from the cut.

Gang Up Boards

The fewer cuts you make with a circular saw, the fewer chances for a mistake to happen. That's why I like to gang up same-size project pieces and cut them all in one swoop. You'll need to spend a little more time preparing for the cut. That means a solid work table and plenty of clamps.

Rip Cuts

 **Page 127** Make Your Own:
Cutting Guide

The most difficult part of making a rip cut is finding a good place to stand while you make the cut. The photo above is a little misleading—normally I would stand *in front* of the sawhorses and push the saw as I walk along the length of the board. Keep in mind that making rip cuts with a circular saw are a little more difficult (and dangerous) than making crosscuts. That's why it's important to prepare a solid work station and make sure that everything is securely clamped before making the cut.

Rip Cut Tips & Tricks

Mark Cut Line

I like to use a combination square to draw a cut line for ripping. First extend the square to match the amount of wood you want to remove. Then follow the edge of the square with a pencil as you slide it along the length of the board.

Clamp it Down

Ripping a board with a circular saw can be a little tricky, but with the right set up, the job can be done without a hitch. Start with a solid work table, bench, or pair of sawhorses, and a set of four clamps to hold everything in place while you cut.

Use a Rip Guide

The only way to get a straight edge with a circular saw is to use a cutting guide. You can buy an aluminum straight edge at a home center, or better yet, make your own panel cutting guide from scrap wood in your shop (see page 127).

bring it all together
Assembly

Learning how to assemble a wood project is probably the most troublesome part of woodworking. It's a critical step that requires near perfection in how you mark screw locations, drill pilot holes, and drive fasteners. One mistake and your project could be ruined entirely. The good news is that with a little patience and planning, assembling a project can be the most rewarding step in the entire process (there's no better feeling than to see your project finally come together!)

In this section, I'll show you some of the more simple and easy methods I've found for joining boards and using fasteners. Because this book focuses on building projects using simple and inexpensive tools, I've purposely avoided some of the more sophisticated (and difficult) joinery techniques that experienced woodworkers might use in the same situation. That said, the techniques I outline here will still give you a tough, solid construction designed to last a lifetime.

Joinery Basics......page 43
Take an inside look at what makes a strong joint, and how to make your project joinery last a lifetime.

Fasteners.................page 45
Discover the two most common methods for bonding wood joints—using glue, wood screws, and a driver.

Pocket Holes.........page 50
Explore this unique option for bringing boards together—using a pocket hole jig and some pocket screws.

Page **Learn More About:**
82 **Drilling Pilot Holes**

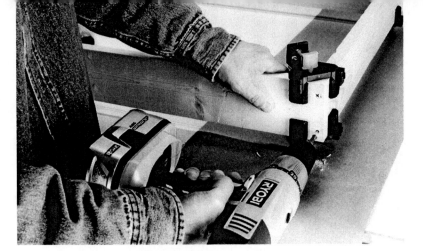

Joinery Basics

Most boards give us three places to form a joint: the face, the edge, and the end. Find out which location provides the strongest bond.

Weak	Stronger	Strongest

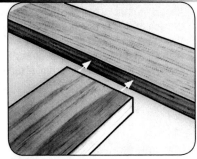

End to End

As practical as it might seem to attach boards at each end, this does not make for a good glue joint. Not that you have to avoid end-to-end joinery entirely, but it does mean the joint may need some extra support—with pocket hole screws, brackets, or cleats.

End to Edge

Using the side of a board in a joint adds a little more bonding strength. However, the total gluing surface is still relatively small, which keeps end-to-edge joints somewhat weak. The solution is to add extra support—with pocket hole screws or brackets.

Face to Face

The large gluing surface makes face-to-face joints (lap joints) actually stronger than the surrounding wood itself. You'll find a lot of variations: lap joints, half-lap joints, mitered half laps, just to name a few. Each take advantage of the abundant gluing surface to create a super-strong bond.

Recommended Joinery:

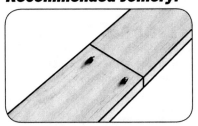

Pocket Hole Joints

Recommended Joinery:

Pocket Hole Joints

Recommended Joinery:

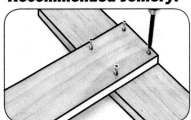

Glue & Screw

Half-Lap Joinery

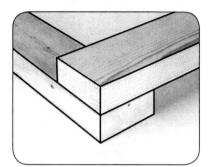

Full-Lap Joint

A full-lap joint is simply one board *face* attached to another. Use glue, nails, or screws, to bond the wood. No fancy cutting needed here, which makes a full lap joint one of the quickest and easiest joints of all to make.

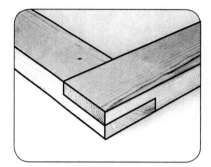

Half-Lap Joint

The challenge in making a half-lap joint is to remove half the thickness of each adjoining board, making sure the gluing surface is perfectly flat and square. That usually requires power tools, like a table saw or a router table.

Sandwich Lap

You can easily create the *effect* of a half-lap joint by "sandwiching" boards together—leaving gaps at the end of the board where the joints are to be located. Locking boards together like this also doubles the overall strength.

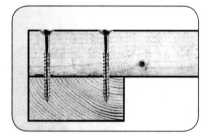

Bring it Together

Glue & screw works fine for most half-lap joinery projects. With larger boards I like to use a tougher fastener—like a carriage bolt or a lag screw.

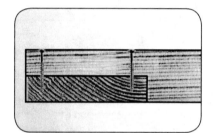

Bring it Together

If you have the tools to make clean half laps, you can skip fasteners entirely and simply glue and clamp the boards together.

Bring it Together

Once you have the board pairs joined with glue and nails (let these dry overnight), complete the joinery with wood screws.

secure the joint
Using Fasteners

The assembly methods I've chosen here are my favorites for quick and easy joinery—and are perfect for people just getting started in the craft. Keep in mind that these are *only a few* of the many possible ways to bring a project together. As you gain more experience, you may want to explore more complex joinery methods.

Page 82 — **Learn More About:**
Drilling Pilot Holes

Glue & Nail ....page 46
Sometimes a hammer and nail is all it takes to assemble a sturdy, well-built project. Keep in mind that the primary purpose of a nail is to work like a clamp, holding project pieces together just long enough for the glue to dry.

Glue & Screw .... page 48
With some projects, you might consider using wood screws instead of nails. Why? Wood screws can offer more strength to the overall structure, and in some cases, are just easier to work with than nails.

Glue & Nail

Some might think using nails is a sloppy way to build a wood project. Truth is, a glue and nail joint (when done properly) is more stable and durable than the surrounding wood itself. My favorite part about glue & nail joinery is the simple two-step process. Once you have the boards lined up, it's a quick job to apply glue and then drive the nails in place.

Getting Started

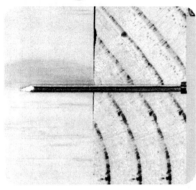

Which Nail?

I like to use a *bright finish* nail for this type of joinery. The nail has a very small head that can be hammered below the surface, and then later hidden with putty. Look for the "4d" size, which is just the right length for joining 1x lumber (¾" thick boards).

How Many Nails?

I like to space nails 3-4 inches apart. Getting them closer won't add strength, and going beyond 4 inches might leave some gaps in the clamping power of a nail. Try using the EZ Pilot Hole Guide template to get nail holes lined up evenly along the edge.

How Much Glue?

I don't mind using a little more glue than is necessary—because too little glue makes a weak joint. Apply a smooth, thick coat that covers the entire edge of the board. When using white and yellow glues, apply glue to *one side* of the joint only.

(Page 149) **Learn More About:**
Nail Sizes

Glue & Nail: Step by Step

① Mark the Spot

Driving nails along the edge of a 1x board can be tricky. That's why I like to use a guide to mark the locations before bringing out the hammer. A common woodworker's awl and the EZ pilot hole guide does the job.

Page Make Your Own
133 Pilot Hole Guides

② Add Glue

You'll need some type of applicator to spread the glue evenly—a paint stir stick, a foam brush, or a piece of stiff paper. Keep in mind that a certain amount of glue will ooze out of the joint when you start nailing the boards together (squeeze out). Actually, squeeze out is a good sign that you'll have a strong joint when it dries. Runny glue can make a big mess, though, so put something under your project to catch the drips. I like to use cheap painter's paper or kitchen wax paper.

③ Nail it

I like to use corner clamps to hold my project pieces together while nailing. However, before driving the first nail, it's a good idea to double check that everything is straight and square. A simple carpenter's square placed along the inside corner of your project will tell you immediately if everything is in order. If not, try using an inexpensive rubber mallet to tap the sides of the project back in alignment. As you drive the nails, stop just short of the surface (use a nail setter to finish, see below).

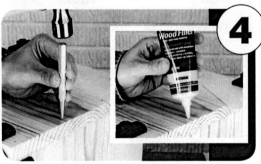

④ Hide it

The head of a finish nail is small enough that you can drive it just below the surface of the wood, and then later hide it completely with wood filler. A nail setting tool lets you do this without marring the surface of the board. Don't go too deep, though. A few taps should be plenty to set the nail just below the surface.

Glue & Screw

Sometimes woodscrews just work better than nails.
Woodscrews can add more strength to a joint, which
can be important for projects that need it—like
furniture and large cabinets. Also, sometimes it's just
easier to drive a screw into a board than hammer in
a nail. Screws are not only more predictable in their
behavior, but usually more accurate too.

Getting Started

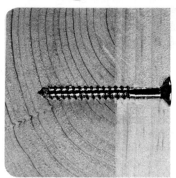

Screw Size?

The primary job of a woodscrew is to
act like a clamp—holding two boards
together just long enough for the glue
to dry. You might be surprised just how
small of a screw will get the job done—
and for less money. See page 82 for
more tips on driving screws.

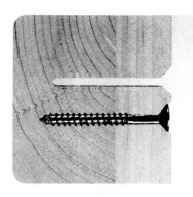

Pilot Hole First?

Although it's possible to drive a screw
without a pilot hole, more often than
not you'll split the board or strip out the
head of the screw. Better to have a set
of countersink bits on hand to avoid
these problems. See page 82 for more
tips on driving screws.

Tame the Torque

Sometimes a drill/driver will send a
screw too far into the board—sometimes
making the screw poke through the
other side. The torque adjustment on
your drill/driver can prevent these kinds
of mishaps. See page 14 for more
about setting torque.

Glue & Screw: Step by Step

Mark the Spot

The ¾" thickness of a 1x board leaves a *very* small target for drilling pilot holes. Getting too close to the edge will cause the screw to split the edge of the board. The EZ Pilot Hole Guides at the back of this book solve the problem.

Page Make Your Own
133 **Pilot Hole Guides**

Add Glue

Find a make-shift applicator to spread the glue evenly—a paint stir stick, a foam brush, or a piece of stiff paper. Keep in mind that a certain amount of glue will ooze out of the joint (squeeze out) when you start screwing the boards together (a good sign that you'll have a strong joint). Runny glue can make a big mess, though, so put something under your project to catch the drips, like cheap painter's paper or kitchen wax paper.

Clamp and Countersink

Once both surfaces are stuck together—and the corner clamps are in place—it's time to drill a countersink pilot hole at each of the locations you marked in step 1. As you drill into the wood, try to keep your drill straight and square to the surface of the board. Be sure to let the countersink bit create a small pocket for the head of the woodscrew, which will sit just below the surface.

Drive Screws

With a properly drilled pilot hole, a woodscrew should go into a board quick, smooth, and easy. If not, this a clear warning that something went wrong during the process leading up to this final step.

Page Learn More About:
82 **Driving Screws**

Pocket Holes

A pocket hole provides a small tunnel for a screw, which allows the screw to pull two boards together with amazing speed and efficiency. Of course you'll need a *pocket hole jig* to make the process work, a tool you can find at most home centers and woodworking supply stores.

Your pocket hole jig will include detailed instructions for setting up the tool and making adjustments to match the size of board you are using. Below is a quick overview of the process.

Learn More About
Pocket Hole Joints
Page **91**

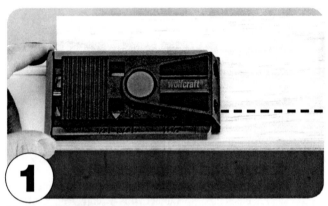

①

Line up first hole—With some boards, you'll need to move the jig from one side to the other to get two pocket holes spaced evenly across the width of the board.

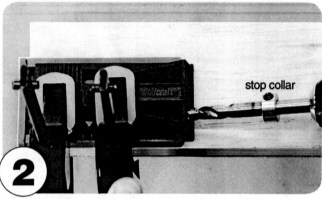

②

Clamp it down—Clamp the jig in place, and then carefully insert the bit into the outermost hole of the jig. Keep drilling till you reach the stop-collar on the bit.

③

Line up for second hole—Move the jig to the opposite side of the board and clamp in place. Insert bit into the outside hole of jig and drill till you reach the stop collar.

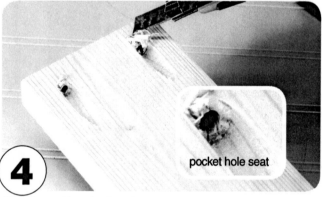

④

Finish up—Note the "seat" your drill bit created inside the pocket. This stops the screw and keeps it from going completely through the board. I like to clean up the rough edges with a utility blade.

how to build anything
Build a Box

The inside structure of most wood furniture starts with a simple box, carcass, and frame.

Plus:
How to Build a Cabinet

how to build a
Solid Wood Box

Once you get started building things from wood, you'll discover that what lies under the surface of most wood furniture is a simple box. As you'll see in the following pages, that box can take a variety of shapes and forms (carcass, frames), but at its core, a box is still a box.

What makes a *solid* wood box unique from other types of box construction is that it doesn't need an inner frame to support its structure. The top, bottom, sides, and back of the box *is* the supporting structure. This makes a solid wood box the perfect starter project for learning to build furniture.

Things You Can Build From a Solid Wood Box

Storage Units
A solid box makes a perfect container, one that can be customized in just about any shape you can imagine.

Bookcases
The most simple bookcase is nothing more than a solid wood box. This style bookcase is made from 1x12 pine.

Cabinets
Cabinets often start out as a simple wood box, with doors and decorative trim added later to the project.

Solid Wood Box Anatomy

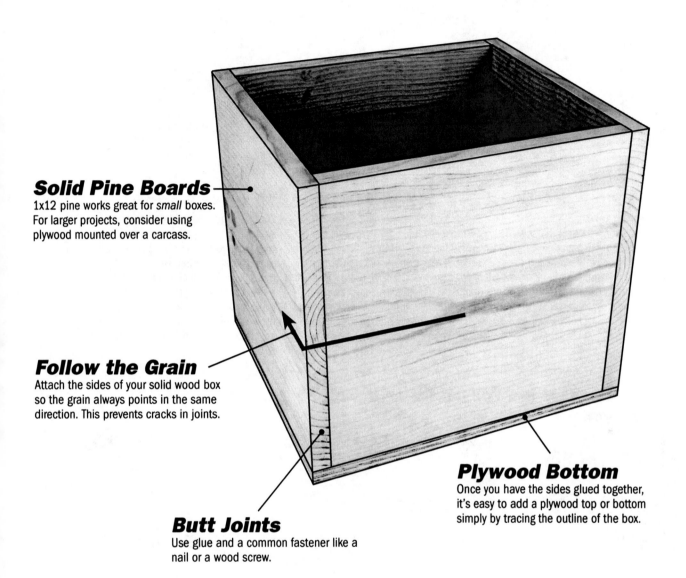

Solid Pine Boards
1x12 pine works great for *small* boxes. For larger projects, consider using plywood mounted over a carcass.

Follow the Grain
Attach the sides of your solid wood box so the grain always points in the same direction. This prevents cracks in joints.

Butt Joints
Use glue and a common fastener like a nail or a wood screw.

Plywood Bottom
Once you have the sides glued together, it's easy to add a plywood top or bottom simply by tracing the outline of the box.

Solid Wood Box: Getting Started

Match Pieces

One of the most important steps in building a solid wood box is making sure all pieces are cut accurately and are consistent in size. With the box I'm building here, the front and back pieces must be identical. Likewise, the side pieces must also match each other perfectly. If not, the box will never be square—or usable.

Dry Assemble First

Before I attach anything together permanently, I like to be sure that everything fits the way it should. I use a set of corner clamps to hold the sides of my box in position, and a carpenter's square to check if the inside corners are square. I'll remove the clamps later to apply glue, and then re-attach them before driving screws.

Keep it Square

It's impossible to hold four pieces of wood in place with two hands. That's why I use corner clamps to temporarily keep things together. They're not tight enough to do real clamping, but they're perfect for keeping boards steady while I work on the joinery. This helps me concentrate on what I need to be concentrating on (driving screws).

Tools You'll Need for Building a Solid Wood Box

Circular Saw
Makes easy cutting of the sides, top and bottom.

Drill & Driver
Must-have tool for building a box using wood screws.

Hammer
Use a light-duty hammer for driving nails in boxes.

Corner Clamps
There's no better way to build a box. Buy a set of 8.

54 | www.ezwoodshop.com

Solid Wood Box: 2 Methods

1

Glue & Nail .... page 56

Sometimes a hammer and nail is all it takes to assemble a sturdy, solid wood box—especially with smaller projects like you see in the photo above. Keep in mind that the primary purpose of a nail is to hold the box together just long enough for the glue to dry.

2

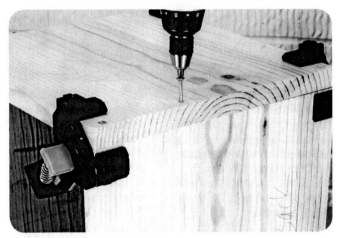

Glue & Screw .... page 59

With some projects you might consider using wood screws to bring everything together. Wood screws offer more strength to the overall structure, and in some cases, are just easier to work with than nails. However, they require a couple extra steps in the process.

Glue & Nail Method

Some might think that using nails is a sloppy way to build a wood project. Truth is, a glue and nail joint (when done properly) is more stable and durable than the surrounding wood itself.

My favorite part about glue & nail joinery is the simple two-step process. Once you have the boards lined up, it's a quick job to apply glue and then drive the nails in place.

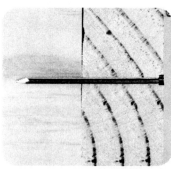

What Size Nail?

I like to use a "bright finish" nail for bringing 1x boards together. The nail has a very small head that can be hammered below the surface, and then later on hidden with putty. Look for the "4d" size, which is just the right length for joining ¾" thick boards.

How Many Nails?

I like to space nails 3-4 inches apart. Getting them closer won't add strength, and going beyond 4 inches might leave some gaps in the clamping power of a nail. Try using the EZ Pilot Hole Guide template (see page 133) to get all of your nail holes lined up evenly.

How Much Glue?

I don't mind using a little more glue than is necessary—since using too little glue might cause the joint to be weak. Apply a smooth, thick coat that covers the entire edge of the board. Also, with white and yellow glues, just add glue to one of the surfaces being joined.

4d Bright Finish

(**Page** **149**) **Learn More About:**
Nail Sizes

Glue & Nail: Step by Step

① Mark the Spot

A nail can easily pierce through the side of a box or split a corner if driven too close to the edge of a board. That's why the first thing I do before assembling a box is determine exactly where I'm going to drive the nails. The EZ Pilot Hole Guide (see below) makes it easy to mark where each nail should go. This is especially important in making sure I hit dead-center on the ¾" board I'm nailing into. A simple woodworking awl is the perfect tool for marking these locations, as well as giving you a small starter hole for the nail itself.

② Add Glue

You'll need some type of make-shift applicator to spread the glue evenly—a paint stir stick, a foam brush, or a piece of stiff paper. I like to work on one side of the box at a time, leaving the corner clamps in place on the opposite side. Keep in mind that a certain amount of glue will inevitably seep out of the joint (squeeze out) and drip on to whatever you're using for a table. Glue can be a sticky mess, so put something under the box to catch drips. Use cheap painter's paper or kitchen wax paper to keep your workstation clean.

Page 133 Make Your Own
Pilot Hole Guides

Glue & Nail: Step by Step

③ Nail it

Once I have both surfaces stuck together—and the corner clamps back in place—I can bring out the hammer and get started. However, I like to first double check that everything is straight and square before driving the first nail. A simple carpenter's square placed along the inside edge of the box will tell me immediately if everything is square. If not, I can use a rubber mallet to tap the sides of the box back in alignment. As you drive the nails into the wood, be careful not to nail too far in. You don't want the head of the hammer to dent the surface of the wood.

④ Hide it

The head of a finish nail is small enough that you can drive it just below the surface, then later hide it completely from view. An inexpensive nail setting tool lets you do this without marring the surface of the board. Don't go too deep, though. A few taps should be plenty to set the nail just below the surface. Later you can hide the hole with a wood filler.

Glue & Screw

Sometimes woodscrews just work better than nails. A woodscrew can add more strength to a joint, which can be important for projects that need it—like furniture and large cabinets. A woodscrew also tends to be a more predictable type of fastener than an ordinary nail, thanks to today's cordless drill/drivers. With the right countersink and pilot hole bit, the glue & screw method can be the quickest and most efficient way to build a wood project.

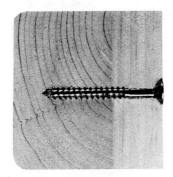

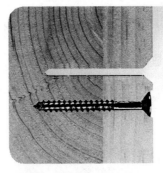

Screw Size?

The primary job of a woodscrew is to act like a clamp—holding two boards together just long enough for the glue to dry. Bigger doesn't always mean better, and you might be surprised just how small of a screw will get the job done—and for less money.

Pilot Hole First

Although it's possible to drive a screw into a board without a pilot hole, more often than not you'll split the edge of the board—or strip out the head of the screw because it just won't budge. Better to have a set of countersink bits on hand to make things easy.

Tame the Torque

Sometimes a drill/driver will send a screw too far into a board—splitting the wood or making the screw poke through the other side. The torque adjustment control on your drill/driver (see page 14) can prevent these kinds of project mishaps from ever happening.

(Page) 82 Learn more about:
Driving Screws

(Page) 11 Learn more about:
Cordless Drills

Speed — Torque

Control the power of your drill!

Glue & Screw: Step by Step

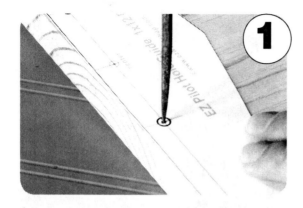

1

Mark the Spot

A woodscrew can easily pierce through the side of a box or split a corner if driven too close to the edge of a board. That's why the first thing I do before assembling a box is determine exactly where I'm going to drill the pilot holes. The EZ Pilot Hole Guide (see below) makes it easy to mark these locations. A simple woodworking awl is the perfect tool for making the marks, as well as giving you a small starter hole for the drill bit to follow.

2

Add Glue

You'll need some type of make-shift applicator to spread the glue evenly—a paint stir stick, a foam brush, or a piece of stiff paper. I like to work on one side of the box at a time, so I'll leave the corner clamps in place on the opposite side. Keep in mind that a certain amount of glue will seep out of the joint (squeeze out) and drip on to whatever you're using for a table. Glue can be a sticky mess, so put something under the box to catch drips. Use cheap painter's paper or kitchen wax paper to keep the worktable clean.

(Page) **133** Make Your Own
Pilot Hole Guides

Glue & Screw: Step by Step

3 Clamp and Countersink

Once I have both surfaces stuck together—and the corner clamps back in place—it's time to drill a countersink pilot hole at each of the locations I marked in step 1. As I drill into the wood, I try to keep my drill pointed level and straight into the board. Later, this will make the woodscrew travel as straight as possible into the adjoining board. Be sure to let the countersink bit dig fairly deep into the surface, making a small pocket for the head of the woodscrew to sit just below the surface.

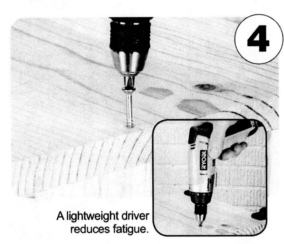

A lightweight driver reduces fatigue.

4 Drive Screws

With a properly drilled pilot hole, a woodscrew should go into a board quick, smooth, and easy. If not, it's a clear warning that something went wrong during process leading up to this final step (see extras: pilot holes and driving screws)

Keep in mind that with small wood projects (like this box), you might prefer using a smaller and more lightweight driver to set the screws. They certainly have enough power to do the job, and can make the task of driving a large number of screws less fatiguing.

Add Top & Bottom

A solid wood box works nice for any number of different wood projects—like storage compartments, shelves, and other things mounted to a wall. However, adding a top and bottom opens up a new world of possibilities for project ideas. An *enclosed* box provides the basic structure for building real furniture—like bookcases, blanket chests, and toy boxes.

The best part is that adding a top and bottom is probably the easiest part of the entire project, thanks to the convenience of plywood panels. Check out the easy steps below for adding a top and bottom to a solid wood box.

① Use Plywood

Plywood is the perfect material for adding a top and a bottom to a solid wood box. And since plywood comes in 4' x 8' panels, there's really no limitation to how large a box you can build.

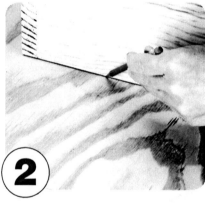

② Trace Outline

No need to measure here. Just sit the box directly on the plywood and trace the outline. When cutting plywood, be sure to use a circular saw cutting guide to get a clean, straight edge for your box.

③ Nail it Down

I like to use small finish nails to attach the plywood top and bottom to my box. You'll need to hit dead center in the ¾" board directly below, otherwise the nail might break through the side.

at the core
Carcass

Sometimes it's just not practical to build a project from a solid wood box, especially with large items like storage cabinets and custom furniture. The wood gets too heavy, too unwieldy, and too expensive. That's why experienced carpenters more often build a wood carcass first, and then use lighter-weight materials to complete the outer appearance of the project.

Things You Can Build with a Wood Carcass

Storage Cabinets

The most economical way to build anything large is to start with a carcass. Since a carcass is often hidden from view by the time the project is finished, you can use less-expensive materials in the construction. I've found that 1x2s and 1x4s make surprisingly strong and durable frameworks, that I can easily cover with a variety of materials to improve the appearance.

Built-In Furniture

Most of the custom carpentry you'll find in a remodeled house begins with a carcass—conveniently hidden underneath the finished appearance. Things like day beds, window seats, and fireplace surrounds usually start with a pine carcass for the underlying construction, which is later covered with hardwood trim and face frames to complete the project.

You Imagine it!

Once you have the knack for building a carcass, the possibilities for projects are limited only by your imagination. Of course, you'll always want to keep strength and durability the primary focus in your design, for the simple sake of making your project safe to use. However, this still leaves plenty of room to explore, discover, and invent new ways to build things.

Carcass Anatomy

Side Rail

Side Rail

Stretchers

Stile

Stile

Tools You'll Need to Build a Carcass

Corner Clamps
The most troublesome part of building a carcass is getting all the boards lined up and ready to drill. Fortunately, this is an easy problem to solve. The corner clamps you see here keep my boards perfectly aligned at 90 degrees, leaving my hands free to handle the drill.

Drill/Driver
A cordless drill is the perfect tool for drilling pilot holes and driving wood screws into the corners of a carcass. Be sure to take advantage of the adjustable torque setting, which will help you avoid driving the screw too far and splitting the wood.

Countersink Bit
The best way to avoid splitting a board when driving screws is to first make a pilot hole. A countersink bit (see photo above) creates the perfect path, and can be adjusted to match the length and shape of the particular woodscrew you are using with your project.

Building a Carcass
Getting Started

As in all things, the *quality* of the end product depends mostly on the *quality* of work you do in the process. That's why it's important to make sure your completed carcass is as straight and square as possible before moving on to the next stage of the project. One way to avoid problems early on is to choose boards from the lumber store that are straight and square to begin with. Take a little extra time at the lumber store to find boards that are free from defects—like bow and twist (see more about choosing lumber on page 25).

Working with Dimensional Lumber

Unfortunately, most of the inexpensive 1x lumber sold at a home center is far from being perfectly straight and square. That's why serious woodworkers own tools like table saws and wood planers, which allow them to fine-tune the shape, width, and length of a board before using it in a project. I won't be covering how to use these more sophisticated tools here, but you can still make sure all your project boards have consistent length with the more simple tools I use in this book.

Consistency is the Key

First take all the like-size project pieces you've cut and line them up on a table. Clamp them together, and then use a small carpenter's square to see just how close the boards match up (see photo right). If one board is noticeably shorter or longer than another, this is the time to address the problem, not later. A rough wood file or a simple sanding block works fine for leveling off high or low spots you find on the ends.

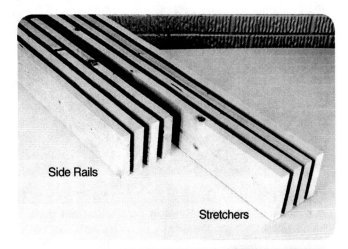

Side Rails

Stretchers

Carcass: Join Rails & Stretchers

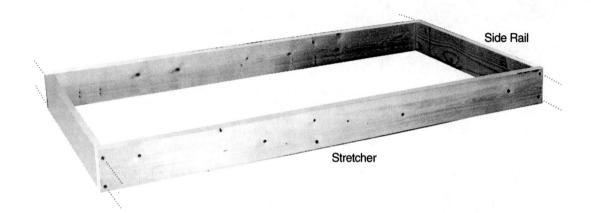

Side Rail

Stretcher

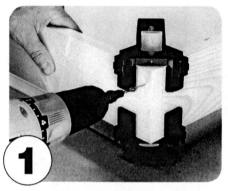

Attach Corner Clamps

Corner clamps do a great job of holding boards together while you complete the joinery. The shape of the clamp automatically forces the two boards to line up at a perfect 90 degree angle. After you complete the joint, just remove the clamps and move them to the next corner. Or simply buy a set of 8 clamps—two for each corner.

countersink pilot holes

Drill Pilot Holes

Pilot holes help prevent boards from splitting when driving screws. However, you'll also need to create a small pocket so the head of the woodscrew can sit just below the surface. I like to use an adjustable countersink bit to accomplish both jobs. The bit cuts a small hole on the surface just large enough for the head of the screw.

Countersink Bit

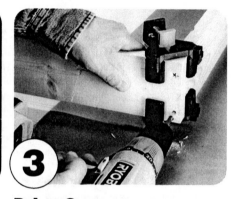

Drive Screws

After getting all the countersink holes drilled, it's time to start driving the screws. Be careful not to drive the screws in too far—this is a quick way to make the board split. Do a little experimenting with the torque adjustment on your drill/driver to find the best setting to drive screws just below the surface, but no farther!

Page 82 Learn more about:
Driving Screws

Carcass: Attach Stiles

Stiles

Stiles

Pocket Hole Joinery

Adding the stiles (vertical boards) gives you a nice sneak-peak at how your finished project will look. However, the joinery for attaching these vertical boards can be a little tricky. That's because we're talking about a fairly weak joint to begin with—attaching the *end* of one board to the *edge* of another.

Most of the problem comes from the fact that there's really no way to attach two boards end-to-edge without bringing in more sophisticated woodworking tools and techniques. That's where *pocket hole joinery* comes to the rescue!

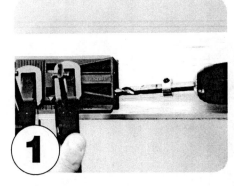

1

2

3

Drill Pockets

With a pocket hole jig and a few accessories, you can create a surprisingly strong joint at the corners of a carcass. That's where it really needs the strength right now, just to hold everything together until you can get some other supporting materials in place (like the plywood sides).

Page 91 Learn more about:
Pocket Holes

Check for Accuracy

The photo above shows what your pocket holes should look like. If the jig is set correctly, your pocket hole bit will create a small protrusion through the end of the board—centered in the thickness of the wood. Experiment on a piece of scrap wood to get a feel for using the jig.

Attach Stiles to Rails

Glue is optional with pocket hole joints, as most builders will tell you the joints are strong enough without it. However, when I'm building a project that demands a little extra strength in the basic structure, I prefer to err on the side of caution and apply some glue before driving in the screws.

how to build
Frames

Frames are so common in wood furniture that most of the time we don't even notice them. Sure, they're easy to spot in cabinet doors and behind family photos, but frames also play an important part in making wood projects more efficient and economical. Here's why:

Cost—Frames are often used to conceal the inside construction (carcass) of a project. That means you can buy less expensive wood for that part of the project (that doesn't show), and buy better quality wood for the frame (that does show).

Efficiency—Furniture rarely needs the bulk, strength, and complexity of solid wood construction. Frame construction makes it possible build simple, lightweight projects using 1x lumber and plywood. This reduces the amount of materials needed to complete the project.

What to Build with Wood Frames

Cabinet Doors

Most cabinet doors start out as a pair of wood frames. How you customize and style the frames can be as simple or complex as you want it to be.

Face Frames

Frames *conveniently* hide the rough edges of a carcass. That means you can buy less expensive wood for what stays hidden, and better wood for what shows.

TOP RAIL

STILE

PANEL

STILE

BOTTOM RAIL

Pocket Holes

Frame Anatomy

Rails, Stiles, and Panels

The terms "rail" and "stile" and "panel" are nothing more than simple naming conventions to identify the components of *frame & panel construction*. In woodworking terminology, rails are the *horizontal* pieces of a frame, stiles are *vertical*. What sits in the middle of the frame is called the *panel*.

In conventional frame construction, the rails and stiles include a small groove or lip cut along the inside edge to hold the panel. However, this kind of joinery requires more sophisticated power tools, like a table saw and router table. Instead, I'll be using a simpler method of attaching a hardboard panel to the back of the frame.

Tools You'll Need to Build a Frame

Pocket Hole Jig

Conventional frame & panel construction requires expensive tools. A pocket hole jig changes all that. You can make super-strong frames using an inexpensive jig and a few tools you already have in the shop.

Drill/Driver

An inexpensive drill/driver covers the job of both drilling pocket holes and driving woodscrews in a frame. Most pocket hole jigs come with their own drill bit and driver. All you need to provide is the power drill itself.

Square

A frame is useless if it's not straight and square. That's why I always keep a *carpenter's square* nearby. Sometimes I'll even clamp the square into the corner of the frame while I work on the joinery.

Getting Started

1 Cut Precise Lengths

The best way to get a frame straight and square is to make sure the boards are the *same length* before you put them together. That means the upper and lower rails are the same length, and the left and right stiles are the same length. Anything less than perfect and your completed frame will be out of square. If you get this right, you'll be amazed at how easy everything else goes together.

2 Lay Out Frame on Table

Once I'm confident that my rails and stiles are perfectly matched, I like to lay everything out on a worktable to see how it fits together. You might discover that some corners don't mesh as well as you'd like them to (cup or twist on a board can aggravate an otherwise smooth and flush joint). First try flipping the boards over find a better fit. Otherwise, sand or plane the surface smooth.

3 Identify Each Piece

If I'm happy with the way everything fits together, I like to mark the boards to remind me where they belong in the frame—top, bottom, left, and right. Be careful what you use to mark up the boards (never use ink or markers). I like to use small adhesive labels, which can be easily peeled off later when the project is finished.

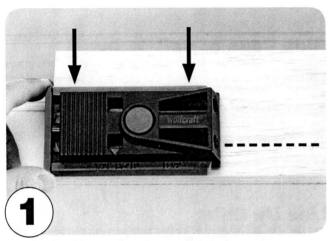

1

Line up first hole—Place the jig flush to one side of the rail (depending on the width of the board, you might need to move the jig to get two pocket holes evenly spaced).

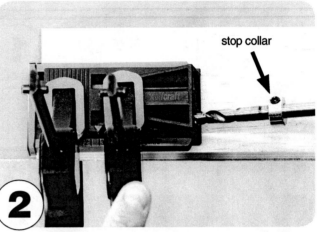

stop collar

2

Clamp it down—Clamp the jig in place, and then carefully insert the bit into the outermost hole of the jig. Keep drilling till you reach the stop-collar on the bit.

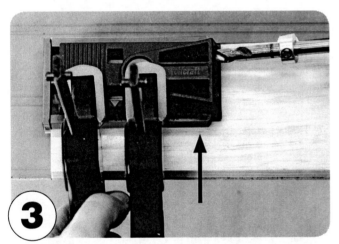

3

Line up for second hole—Move the jig to the opposite side of the board and clamp in place. Insert bit into the outside hole of jig and drill till you reach the stop collar.

4

pocket hole seat

Finish up—Note the flat "seat" your drill bit created inside the pocket. This keeps the screw from going through the board. Clean up rough edges with a blade.

Building a Frame
Attach Rails to Stiles

(1) ### Glue Edge of Rail

Although it's not *always* necessary to glue a pocket hole joint (pocket hole joinery is that strong!) a little glue can ensure the joint will *never come apart*. Don't worry about putting glue on both sides of the joint—a thick layer of glue on one board only will do the job fine.

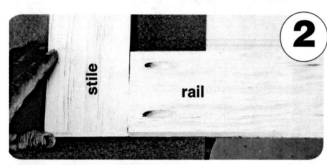

(2) ### Line Up Stile

Find the stile you designated for this particular rail and bring it up snug to the joint. I like to use my fingers to feel along the side of the board and make sure the stile is lined up flush along the bottom.

(3) ### Add Face Board Leveler

Driving pocket hole screws is a one-shot process. That means you'll need to make sure the stile and rail are perfectly aligned with each other on all sides—including the face of the board. I like to clamp a small piece of scrap wood over the two boards keep everything flat while I'm driving the pocket screws.

(4) ### Clamp & Drive Pocket Screws

If I'm happy with the alignment of the rail and stile (double check this to be sure) it's time to drive the pocket hole screws in place. Be careful not to drive the screw too far in the tunnel—this can easily split the edge of the board, or make the screw poke through the underside side of the stile.

Build a Cabinet

Now it's time to transform your completed carcass into a real piece of furniture.

A carcass can easily become the underlying structure for an endless variety of wood projects—the most common being a simple cabinet. Cabinet makers often use carcass & frame construction to save money on materials, using less-expensive wood for the inner structure (which stays hidden from view), and better quality wood for the components that show.

Add Side Panels

I like to use ¼" plywood to cover the top, sides, and bottom of my carcass. It's cheap and easy to cut............page 74

Add a Shelf

A carcass makes it easy to add a shelf to the basic cabinet. I like to use simple glue and nail construction.......page 75

Add Doors

Once you get the hang of making cabinet doors, you'll have the confidence to build almost anything from wood.........page 76

Building a Cabinet
Side Panels

Here I'm attaching plywood to the left and right sides of the cabinet. This not only gives shape to the box, but accounts for most of the strength in cabinet construction.

Side Panel

Trace Edge of Carcass

I like to use ¼" plywood to cover the outer surface of my cabinet. To avoid mistakes in measuring, I simply trace the outline of the carcass directly on top of the sheet of plywood.

Glue & Nail

I like to use ¾" finish trim nails—which are just long enough to hold the plywood panel in place while the glue dries. Use a nail punch to drive the head just below the surface—but no farther!

Patch Nail Holes

If you plan to finish the cabinet with paint, patch the nail holes with wood filler. Fill the hole, then smooth it off flush with a putty knife. Let dry overnight before sanding.

Shelf

Add a Shelf

A box of small finish nails is all you need to attach a plywood shelf to the carcass.

1

Trace Bottom Edge
Use ¼" plywood again for the bottom shelf. First slip the panel under the carcass and let your pencil follow the contour completely around the case.

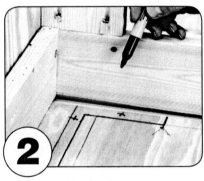

2

Cut Away Corners
To get the bottom shelf to fit inside the carcass, you'll need to cut away a small section at each corner of the panel. This provides room for the vertical rails.

3

Drop Shelf into Place
Don't expect a perfect fit with your first try. You might need to cut away a little more plywood at each corner. Gluing is optional, but can help improve strength.

Building a Cabinet
Add Doors

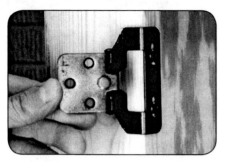

I like to use wrap-around cabinet hinges. They make the job of attaching cabinet doors quick and easy.

Start with the Hinge

One way to make sure doors fit a cabinet is to mount the hinges *first,* then build the doors to fit around the hinges.

This lets you custom-fit the rails and stiles to the exact space available. You'll find plenty of choices for hinges at your home center, but I've found the *wrap-around cabinet hinge* style to be the easiest to install.

Choose Location

Take a look at other cabinets around your home to see where the hinges are located and how they are attached.

There's no right or wrong place to mount a hinge—as long as you are consistent on both sides of the cabinet. Use a carpenter's square to record the location of your first hinge. You'll use this measurement to line up the other hinges.

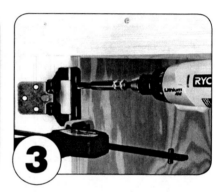

Attach Hinge to Case

Hinges are notorious for moving around while you try to mount them. Here are the tools I use to avoid the problem:

Irwin® Quick-Clamp®—A clamp holds the hinge snug to the carcass while you drive screws.

Self-Centering Drill Bit—This ensures that the pilot hole is perfectly centered in the hinge hole.

Self-centering Bit

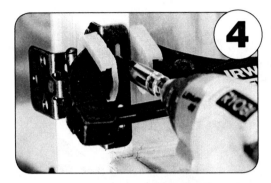

④ Attach Remaining Hinges

Mount the remaining three hinges, using the first hinge location as a guide. As I mentioned earlier, I like to use an adjustable square to note the position of my first hinge and then copy that measurement to the other hinge locations around the cabinet.

⑤ Find Height for Frame Stile

With all four hinges mounted, you can now start building the doors. I like to begin by deciding just how tall of a door I want for the cabinet. Look at some of the cabinets around your home to get ideas. In my example, I decided to keep the door about an inch down from the top, in case I decide to add some decorative trim later. Once you're happy with your chosen door size, cut four frame stiles to the same length.

⑥ Line Up Frame Stiles

Now clamp the frame stiles in place directly on the cabinet. Make sure all stiles are pushed snug against the hinges and the tops are lined up square and level across the front of the cabinet. The critical step here is to make sure you allow a small vertical gap where the doors meet in the center. Otherwise, the doors won't close properly. Shoot for a gap around 1/8"—but no larger.

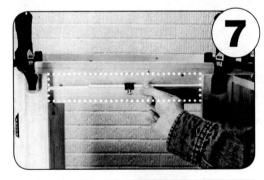

⑦ Find Rail Length

With all the frame stiles clamped in place, you can now get an accurate measurement for the rails. Don't bother trying to measure this space with a ruler. Instead use a simple story stick to copy the distance from the cabinet over to your cutting table. I made the story stick you see here from two small pieces of wood with an office paper clip in the middle (or see my EZ StoryStick below). This method is much easier, quicker, and more accurate than using a ruler.

EZ STORY STICK

www.ezwoodshop.com/ezstorystick.html

Add Doors

8 Mark and Cut Rails

Using the measurement you took with the story stick, cut four matching rails exactly the same length. I like to use my adjustable square to draw perfectly square cut lines across the face of the boards.

9 Assemble & Check Square

With all the rails and stiles cut to size, lay everything out on an assembly table. Line up the pieces as they will appear on the cabinet, and then double check that everything is straight and square. If one corner doesn't seem to line up as well as another, try switching a few boards around to find a better fit.

10 Complete Pocket Hole Joinery

Congratulations! The rails and stiles are cut and laid out in nice, square frames. Now it's time to assemble the frame with pocket hole joinery.

Page 91 Learn more about:
Pocket Holes

11 Smooth Out Edges

After completing your frames, chances are that some of your rails and stiles will not line up perfectly to each other. No problem, really. A little sanding around the problem areas will remove any low or high spots that might be present.

Add Panels

The final step in building a cabinet door is to attach a panel to the back side of the frame. I won't attempt the more traditional technique of frame & panel construction (with rabbet and groove joinery), but instead I'll attach a simple backer made of 1/8" hardboard to enclose the cabinet.

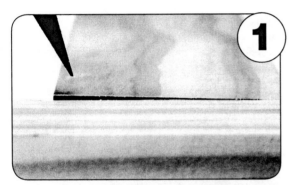

Check for Uneven Joints

If your frame construction is not perfectly flat and square, you might be left with a corner joint that has a raised edge (see photo at left). This can cause some trouble when you try to attach a hardboard panel to the frame later on. The problem that can be easily corrected with a little sandpaper and some muscle power. For larger gaps, consider using hand plane to level both sides of the joint.

Mark & Cut Hardboard Panel

The easiest way to create a hardboard panel perfectly matched to your frame is to trace the outline directly on top of the hardboard. Go ahead and use the factory-cut edge of your hardboard panel for as many sides of your frame as you can, which will save you a few cuts.

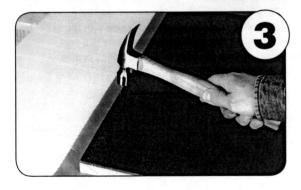

Attach Panel to Frame

Once you have the panel cut to size, it's simply a matter of attaching it to the back of the frame. With 1/8" hardboard, I like to use ½" finish nails spaced about 3" apart. Most woodworkers avoid using glue in this step, to allow for the natural expansion and contraction of wood over time (due to changes in humidity).

Building a Cabinet
Mount Doors

With the frame & panel doors completed, it's time to mount them to the cabinet. The hinges are already in place, so this step should go fairly smooth and easy.

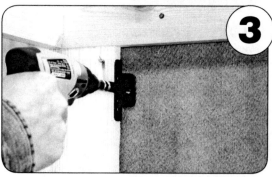

① Position Doors on Cabinet

Clamp the completed doors against the front of the cabinet, snug against the hinges. Carefully nudge the doors up or down to make the them aligned evenly across the top of the cabinet.

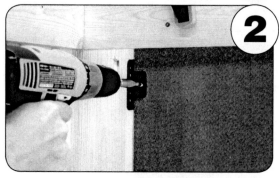

② Drill Pilot Holes in Door

With the hinges already attached to the cabinet, the next step is to attach the doors to the hinges. Find the mounting screws that came with the hinges and locate a drill bit properly matched for that size of screw (see extras: Pilot Holes). Go in from the back of the cabinet and drill a small pilot hole through the mounting hole in the hinge and into the side of the cabinet.

③ Drive Screws

Finish attaching the doors by driving screws that came with the hinges. Be careful not to put too much horsepower into this task—you could easily strip out the pilot holes you drilled in step 2. That's why I like to use a smaller, compact driver when working with hinges.

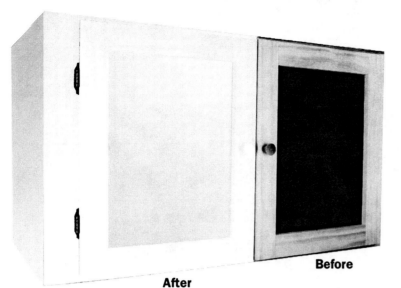

After **Before**

Building a Cabinet
Finishing

Once you have the basic cabinet assembled, there's really no limit to what you can do next to customize the piece to your own taste. For simple shop cabinets in the garage or basement, I don't mind leaving the wood unfinished. However, a nice coat of paint and some decorative knobs can go a long way in making your project look more professional. Below are a few ideas for improving the appearance of your cabinet.

Sand it Smooth

For the super-rough spots, you'll need 80-grit sandpaper to even make a dent in the surface. This is especially true for the corner joints that maybe didn't go together as smooth as you would have liked. After that, I usually run 100-grit sandpaper over the entire project to prepare the wood for painting. To get a super-smooth surface, you might try a final go-over with 220 grit sandpaper.

Don't forget to lightly smooth off the corner edges of all boards. Otherwise they can easily splinter or chip off over time.

Seal & Paint

One of the easiest ways to improve the overall appearance of your cabinet is to simply add a good coat of paint (or two). The problem is that unfinished pine will soak up paint like a sponge. Even after several coats, you might still see knots and other defects showing through the paint.

The best solution is to first apply a shellac-based combination primer and sealant—*before* painting. Although the directions might suggest one coat only, I like to put down two.

Sealer/Primer

Latex Paint

Page 99 **Learn more about:**
Finishing Pine

how to build anything
Drilling & Driving

Easily avoid the most common mistakes made in bringing project pieces together.

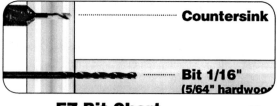

Countersink

Bit 1/16"
(5/64" hardwoo

Plus: Pocket Hole Joints

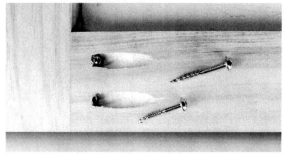

wood screws

pocket hole screws

finish nails

fasten joints with
Nails & Screws

You'll find hundreds of different fasteners on the shelf at your local home center. With so many choices, how can you know which to buy?

As much as I like variety in hardware, the zillions of choices I see in stores confuse me more than help. What I've learned over the years is that most wood projects require only few types of nails and screws to get the job done. Check out the following pages for my complete list of must-have fasteners.

The Only Fasteners You Really Need

4d Finish Nails

Nails are perfect for small wood projects. Drive the narrow head just below the surface of the board, and then cover with a wood filler.

Wood Screws

For larger projects, I use wood screws for easy assembly and rock-solid joinery. Glue is optional—but it's something I recommend for most projects.

Pocket Screws

There's really no substitute for the simplicity (and economy) of pocket hole joints—especially when building frames and cabinets.

Lag Screws

Lag screws give you super strength for the big jobs. Plus, the wide head makes it easy to remove the screws and take apart the project for storage.

Use them for

Easy Assembly

Use finish nails to build small boxes, mount plywood, and attach trim. Nails work like a clamp—holding pieces together while the glue dries.

Use them for

Sturdy Joinery

I like to use screws for corner joints when building a box or cabinet—just to add some strength to what is typically the "weakest link" in a project.

Use them for

Easy Frames

Pocket holes make it easy to build the inside framework for all types of cabinets and furniture—without having to use expensive shop tools.

Use them for

Heavy Joints

Some projects call for tougher hardware than a typical nail or screw—especially if it's something you might want to take apart later.

how to drill
Pilot Holes

Most of the problems related to driving screws have nothing to do with the screw itself, but everything to do with the pilot hole (or lack of). The fact is, most wood screws are too large to be forced into a board without some type of path to lead the way. Although they're tempting to ignore, pilot holes can mean the difference between project success—or project disaster.

What Size Pilot Hole Should I Drill?

root   bit

As a general rule, a pilot hole should be the same diameter as the *root* of the screw—the area just below the threads. This allows the bulk of the screw to easily enter a board without splitting the grain, while the threads pull the boards together to form the joint.

Countersink

A Better Fit

A simple pilot hole might be fine for the threaded portion of the screw, but it won't provide any space for the head or the shank (see photo below). The solution is to use a *countersink bit*, which creates both a pilot hole for the threads, and a larger hole for the head and shank.

Tapered or Straight?

Some screws have a shank that is wider than the threaded portion of the screw. That's when I like to use a *tapered* countersink to get the best fit. For screws that have a more narrow shank, I like to use a *straight* countersink bit.

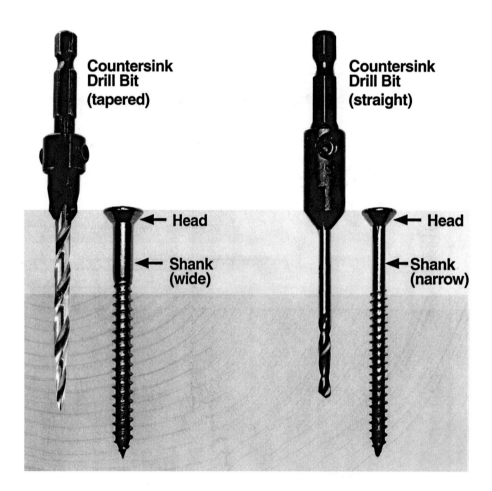

Countersink Drill Bit (tapered)

Countersink Drill Bit (straight)

← Head

← Shank (wide)

← Head

← Shank (narrow)

Driving Nails

Some might frown at using nails to build a wood project, but don't underestimate the power of this incredibly simple and inexpensive fastener.

The real strength in a woodworking joint comes from the glue—*not the fastener*. That means the primary job of a fastener is to simply hold boards together just long enough for the glue to set. For many projects, a 4d finish nail can be the perfect fastener for getting this job done.

4d Finish Nails

Top 3 Mistakes Driving a Nail

Bent Nail
Sometimes it's simply a defective nail. But after the third try, you can bet that something else is wrong.

How to Avoid
- Drill pilot hole first
- Avoid knots in wood
- Check for obstructions

Toe-Nail
Carpenters often use this method to join 2x4 studs, but on small wood projects it can be a disaster.

How to Avoid
- Don't drive a bent nail
- Drill a pilot hole first
- Improve your aim

Dents
A hammer can easily damage a piece of soft pine—leaving a noticeable indent on the surface.

How to Avoid
- Use a nail setter
- Be more gentle
- Improve your aim

EZ Match Chart: Nails

---- BOOK CUTOUT: See page 149

1x FACE JOINT

3d Nail (1¼")

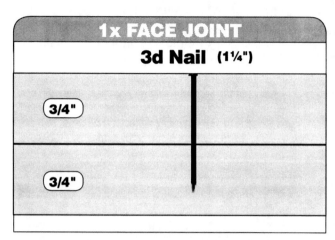

3/4"

3/4"

1x END JOINT

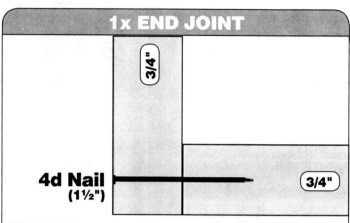

3/4"

4d Nail (1½")

3/4"

1x FACE JOINT

2d Nail (1")

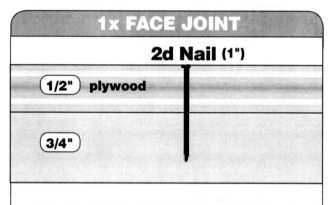

1/2" plywood

3/4"

1x END JOINT

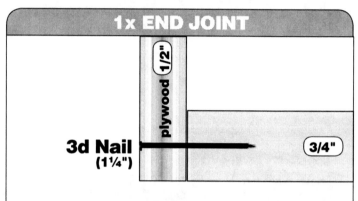

plywood 1/2"

3d Nail (1¼")

3/4"

2x FACE JOINT

8d Nail (2½")

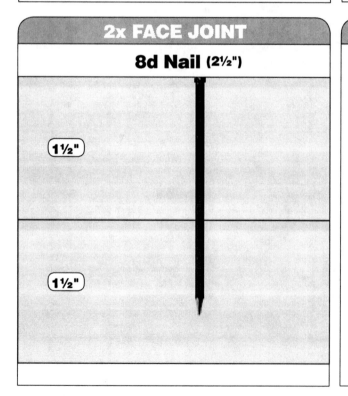

1½"

1½"

2x END JOINT

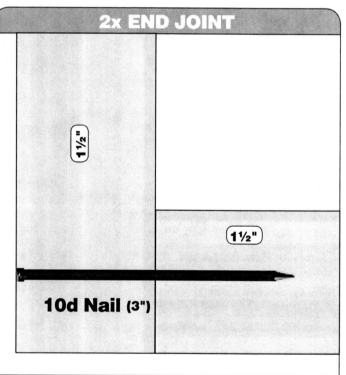

1½"

1½"

10d Nail (3")

Driving Screws

Stop Fighting Screws!

There's nothing more frustrating than having to fight a wood screw during the final stages of a wood project. Screws can be unpredictably stubborn—causing a host of problems in bringing two boards together. The good news is that most of the trouble with driving screws can be blamed on just a few culprits—things that can be easily avoided if you correctly prepare a board for the joint. See the chart below for some of my favorite tips & tricks.

Top 3 Mistakes Driving Screws

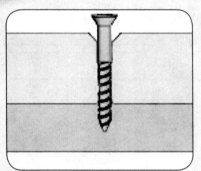 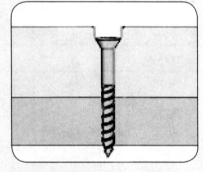 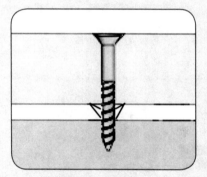

Stalled Screw

Here's where the screw seems to be going in, but suddenly stops short. You can try pushing harder, but you might end up stripping the head—or worse, splitting the board.

Possible Culprit
- No pilot hole
- Pilot hole too small

Cure
First, carefully back the screw out of the board. Then test a larger size pilot hole on a piece of scrap wood. In most cases, it's the shank of the screw that's being stubborn—which can easily be fixed by making a new pilot hole using a tapered countersink bit.

Over-Drive

This is an easy mistake to make with soft wood like pine and poplar. Going in too far can cause the screw to break through the underside of the board you are attaching.

Possible Culprit
- Drill torque set too high
- Pilot hole too large

Cure
Keep in mind that getting the right size pilot hole means you can easily drive a screw too far in—if you're not careful. That's where the adjustable torque setting on your driver comes to the rescue. Also check that your pilot hole is not too large for the screw.

Bridging

Sometimes driving a screw can force boards to separate at the joint, preventing glue from making a solid bond. Unfortunately, it's difficult to see the problem when it's happening.

Possible Culprit
- Boards are warped
- Splinters are blocking joint

Cure
Slightly warped boards can leave a gap in the joint. An easy fix is to tightly clamp the boards together before driving screws. The problem can also be avoided by drilling a countersink in the adjoining board—to keep the splinters from blocking the joint.

EZ Match Chart: Bit & Screw

✂---- **BOOK CUTOUT: See page 151**

1x FACE JOINT

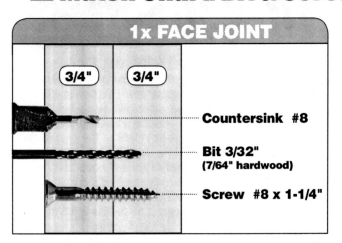

3/4"   3/4"

Countersink #8

Bit 3/32"
(7/64" hardwood)

Screw #8 x 1-1/4"

1x END JOINT

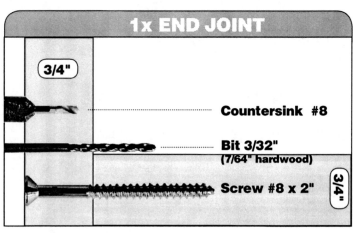

3/4"

Countersink #8

Bit 3/32"
(7/64" hardwood)

Screw #8 x 2"

3/4"

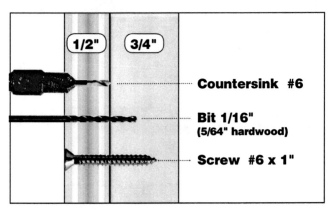

1/2"   3/4"

Countersink #6

Bit 1/16"
(5/64" hardwood)

Screw #6 x 1"

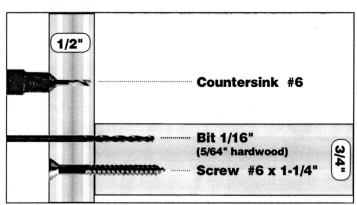

1/2"

Countersink #6

Bit 1/16"
(5/64" hardwood)

Screw #6 x 1-1/4"

3/4"

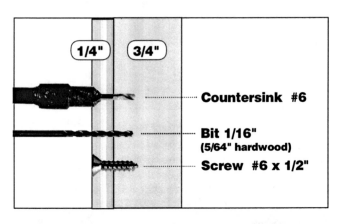

1/4"   3/4"

Countersink #6

Bit 1/16"
(5/64" hardwood)

Screw #6 x 1/2"

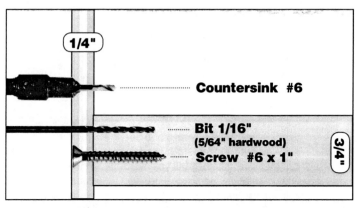

1/4"

Countersink #6

Bit 1/16"
(5/64" hardwood)

Screw #6 x 1"

3/4"

2x FACE JOINT

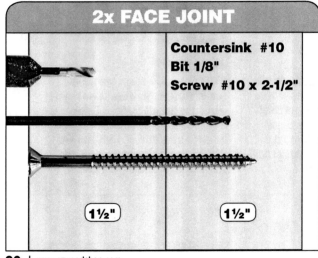

Countersink #10
Bit 1/8"
Screw #10 x 2-1/2"

1½"   1½"

2x END JOINT

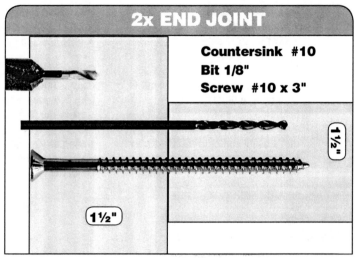

Countersink #10
Bit 1/8"
Screw #10 x 3"

1½"

1½"

Pocket Holes

Make super-strong joints in frames, boxes, cabinets, and custom furniture.

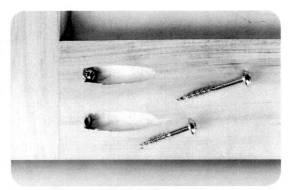

Overview ....page 92

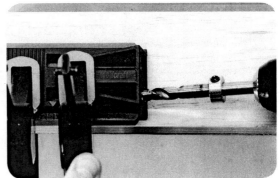

Step by Step ....page 95

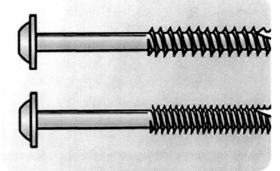

Pocket Screws ....page 97

Pocket Hole Joints

Pocket hole joints provide a super-strong bond between two sides of a board that are typically difficult to join: a **board edge** and a **board end.** Joints like this usually require expensive woodworking tools to make them work—like biscuit jointers and doweling machines. A pocket hole joint changes all that, doing the job faster and cheaper.

How it Works: A pocket hole is like a small tunnel, guiding the pocket screw at an angle through two boards. You'll need a **pocket hole jig**—along with a power drill and a few pocket hole accessories. Glue is optional, as some builders will tell you that pocket hole joints are strong enough without it. However, when I'm building the inner structure of a project (like a cabinet), I use glue to give it some added strength.

POCKET HOLE JOINT: SIDE VIEW

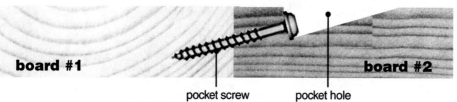

board #1 board #2

pocket screw pocket hole

Things You Can Build with Pocket Hole Joinery

Face Frames
Pocket hole joinery lets you make cabinet face frames quick and easy—and without expensive shop tools.

Cabinet Carcass
Sometimes it's hard to find a spot to join cabinet rails and stretchers. Pocket holes solve the problem.

Solid Wood Boxes
Pocket holes bring the sides of a solid wood box together fast and easy. No fancy joinery or tools needed.

Solid Wood Box

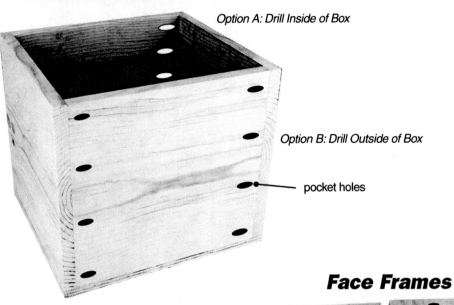

Option A: Drill Inside of Box

Option B: Drill Outside of Box

pocket holes

Face Frames

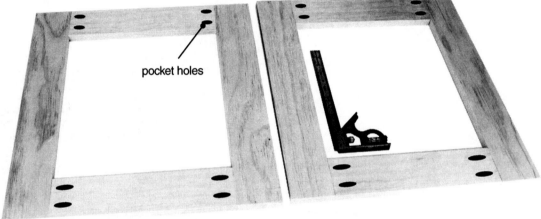

pocket holes

Carcass

Option B: Drill Outside of Carcass

Option A: Drill Inside of Carcass

Pocket Hole Joints

Butt Joints

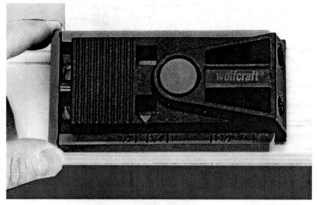

the magic machine
Pocket Hole Jig

Coming from the factories of mass-produced furniture, the pocket hole jig is now a fairly common tool in home workshops. And for good reason. Pocket hole joinery makes furniture building accessible to anyone who can use a power drill and a few common hand tools found at a home center.

Last time I checked, pocket hole jigs range in price from $40 to $150—depending on brand and the type of accessories included in the kit. I've found that the smaller, less-expensive kits work fine, especially if you already have some parts of the kit in your shop (like clamps).

Wolfcraft Jig
Wolfcraft makes a nice-quality pocket hole jig at a very reasonable price.

Kreg Jig
The original maker of pocket hole jigs offers a wide variety of accessories.

Other Tools You'll Need to Make Pocket Hole Joints

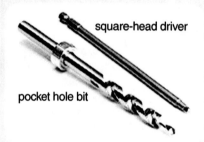

square-head driver

pocket hole bit

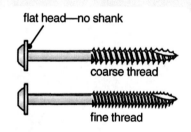

flat head—no shank

coarse thread

fine thread

Power Drill
A simple drill/driver works *reasonably* well for making pocket holes. However, this will put a fair amount of strain on your drill's motor—and battery. A corded drill (if you have one) may be a better choice.

Bit & Driver
Most pocket hole kits include the required bit and driver needed for your drill (an ordinary drill bit won't work). The special pocket hole bit creates a small "seat" at the entrance of the pilot hole.

Pocket Screws
Pocket screws feature a head with a flat underside (see illustration above). Don't try to use a common woodscrew—the beveled shank will either split the board, or keep the screw from seating properly.

This is how your completed pocket holes should look.

Step 1: Drill Pocket Holes

Before you get started, be sure to set your pocket hole to fit the board thickness you're working with. Check the instructions that came with your jig to find out how to make this adjustment. Most pocket hole jigs have two pilot holes, which are spaced perfectly for narrow boards like 1x4s. For wider boards, you'll need to reposition the jig for each hole that you drill (see below).

1 Line Up First Hole

Place the jig flush against one side of your work piece in preparation for the first hole.

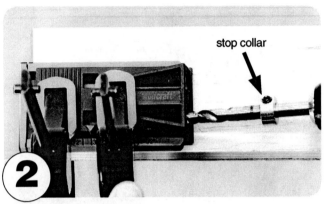

stop collar

2 Clamp it Down

Secure the jig with clamps. Insert bit and keep drilling till you reach the stop-collar on the bit.

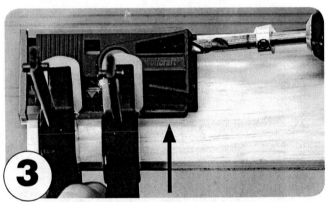

3 Line Up Second Hole

Now move the jig to the opposite side of board. Insert bit and drill till you reach the stop collar.

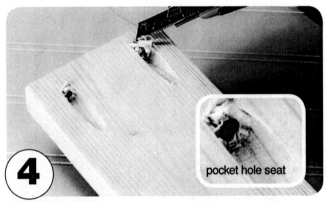

pocket hole seat

4 Finish Up

Note the "seat" created inside the pocket—where the pocket screw will come to a stop. Clean up any rough edges with a utility blade.

Step 2: Drive Pocket Screws

Driving pocket hole screws is a ***one-shot operation***—which means you usually don't have a second chance to correct a misguided screw. That's why it's important to make sure your boards are aligned flat, square, and clamped securely in place before starting. See below for step-by-step instructions.

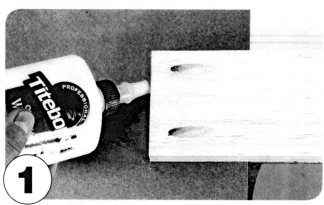

Glue Edge
Although not ***always*** necessary, adding glue to one side of the pocket hole joint will guarantee a permanent bond.

Line Up Boards
I use my eyes and fingers to get everything lined up flush before moving on to the next step.

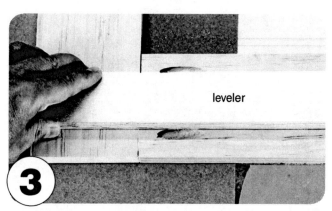

Add Face Board Leveler
Clamp a small piece of scrap wood over the top of both boards to keep them level and flush.

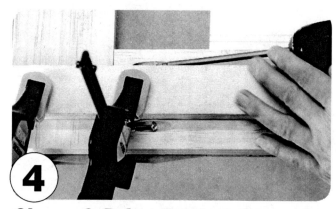

Clamp & Drive Pocket Screws
Drive the screw till you reach the pocket hole "seat" just below the surface—but no farther.

---- **BOOK CUTOUT: See page 153**

HORIZONTAL POCKET JOINTS

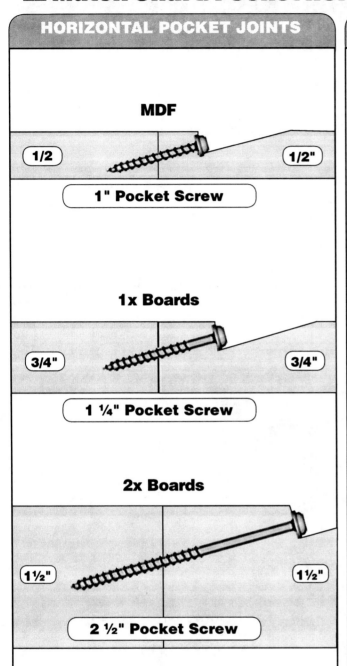

MDF

1/2   1/2"

(**1" Pocket Screw**)

1x Boards

3/4"   3/4"

(**1 ¼" Pocket Screw**)

2x Boards

1½"   1½"

(**2 ½" Pocket Screw**)

VERTICAL POCKET JOINTS

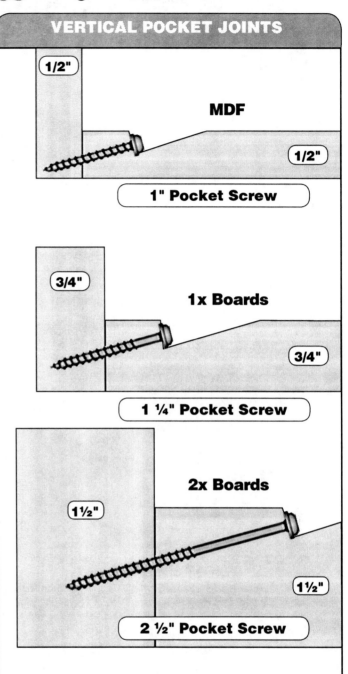

1/2"

MDF

1/2"

(**1" Pocket Screw**)

3/4"

1x Boards

3/4"

(**1 ¼" Pocket Screw**)

1½"

2x Boards

1½"

(**2 ½" Pocket Screw**)

Pocket Screw Chart (all sizes)

Board	Screw Size	Board	Screw Size
1/2" (13mm)	1" (25mm)	1-1/8" (29mm)	1-1/2" (38mm)
5/8" (16mm)	1" (25mm)	1-1/4" (32mm)	2" (51mm)
3/4" (19mm)	1-1/4" (32mm)	1-3/8" (35mm)	2" (51mm)
7/8" (22mm)	1-1/2" (38mm)	1-1/2" (38mm)	2-1/2" (64mm)
1" (25mm)	1-1/2" (38mm)		

Coarse or Fine?

Use coarse-thread pocket hole screws with softwoods—like pine and plywood. Use fine-thread screws with hardwoods—like oak, maple, walnut, and cherry.

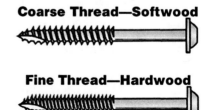

Coarse Thread—Softwood

Fine Thread—Hardwood

Pocket Hole Troubleshooter

Oops...Too Far In!

One of the easiest mistakes to make with pocket hole joinery is to drive the screw so far in that it breaks through the other side. This can be caused by a couple things—either the screw is too long, or the jig was not correctly aligned when you drilled the hole.

EZ Fix...

First, put your drill in reverse and remove the screw. If you've determined the problem is the screw size, replace it with another pocket screw that is at least ¼" shorter than what you pulled out. Next, sand off the damaged area and patch with wood filler.

Oops...Pocket Blowout!

Driving a pocket screw can sometimes break a small chip from the surface of a board. This can also happen if you're attempting to use a *standard* wood screw instead of a pocket hole screw, which won't work with the pilot hole you've created.

EZ Fix...

The easy solution is to do a simple glue & patch repair. You can use the broken chip itself as a patch material, since it should fit the hole perfectly. Fill the hole with glue, and then put the chip back where it belongs.

how to build anything
Finishing Pine

Pine can be stubborn and difficult to finish, unless you know a few tricks.

Clear

Stain

Paint

Milk Paint

Shellac

Do I Really Need a Finish?

As much as I like the look of pine right after sanding, I know that applying a finish is the best way to make my project last. Why? For starters, a finish keeps wood from shrinking and expanding every time the weather changes—which can pull joints apart in just a few weeks. This kind of wood movement can't be eliminated entirely, but a finish will help keep the problem in check. Plus, applying a finish is just good way to protect wood from dust, dirt, and spills.

Page 120 Learn More About:
Toxicity in Finishes

3 EZ Finishes for Pine

Clear
Sometimes the natural color of pine is the perfect look for a project. A clear coat makes finishing quick and easy.

Stain
Stain shows off the grain patterns in wood, and at the same time adds color to your project. Today you'll find lots of color choices.

Paint
Nothing hides mistakes like a solid coat of paint. I like to use a roller with the final coat to get a super-smooth surface.

Water vs Oil

Although some project builders seem to *love* oil-base paints, I can't think of any good reason to use them—other than to cover the bottom of a boat. Water-base* paints do a fine job of protecting wood, and in many cases, are better suited for the project than oil-base paints.

VOCs

If not handled correctly, finishes with high VOCs (volatile organic compounds) can be hazardous to your health and the environment. Use low-VOC finishes when possible.

*For the sake of simplicity, I use the more common term **water-base** in place of **water-borne**, which is a more technically correct term for water-base finishes that dry hard and repel water.*

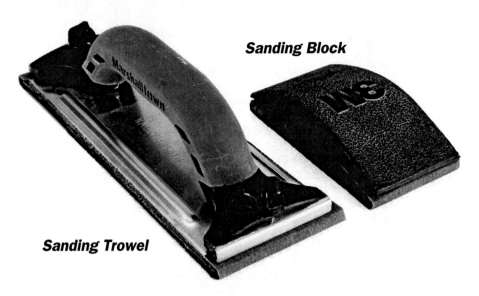

Sanding Block

Sanding Trowel

Sanding

Sanding a wood project can be as simple as spending 5 minutes just to catch the rough spots—or as complex as spending an entire afternoon to get a glass-smooth surface.

The type of sanding I talk about in this book falls somewhere between those two extremes, and is more than adequate when building simple projects for around the home.

1 #60

The Dirty Work

The toughest sanding work you'll do on a wood project is around the joinery, where the edges might not match up perfectly. First see if you can level things off with 60-grit sandpaper. If it's just too much wood to remove, consider using a hand plane or a wood rasp first, then go back with sandpaper.

2 #100

Smooth-Over

Most boards from a home center are fairly smooth to begin with, so all you need at this step is a way to remove built-up dirt and grime. Start with 100-grit sandpaper and cover all the surfaces using a smooth back and forth motion (with the grain). Then repeat the process with 150 grit.

3 #150

Tame Sharp Edges

The last step I take when sanding pine is to remove sharp corners along the edges of my boards. If left alone, these can crack and splinter. Use 150-grit sandpaper, but go lightly. If you see a noticeable bevel, you've sanded too much. This sanding step should be nearly undetectable.

Cut

Cut

(Scrap)

Sanding Trowel

The big handle on a drywall sanding trowel is perfect for sanding wood projects. A standard 9x11 sheet of sandpaper will give you two full pieces for a trowel.

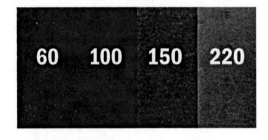

60   100   150   220

Which Grit?

For finishing pine, I like to use four different grits: #60 for rough work around joints, #100 and #150 on board faces, and #220 between coats of paint and multiple layers of clear finish.

Seal Knots in Pine

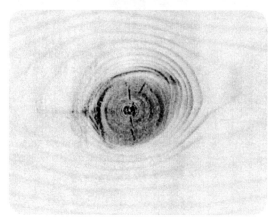

Knots in pine can be tough to seal. Both oil-base and water-base sealers usually fail.

Leaky knots in pine have plagued furniture builders for centuries. We can talk about products that keep knots hidden under a finish (like shellac), or we can talk about avoiding the problem all together. Let's start by looking at some of the more simple approaches to the problem.

Don't Buy Boards with Knots. Or at least find boards that have as few knots and defects as possible. You'll have to do some digging around in the lumber stack—as other shoppers before you have likely done the same thing. You might also consider spending a little more money on clear grade pine or poplar—both of which should be free of knots and defects.

Seal Knots with Glue. Some builders attempt to seal knots by coating them with epoxy glues. Although epoxy might do the job of permanently sealing the resin inside the knot, the glue will leave a raised bump on the surface of your board, which might be difficult sand.

Use a Shellac-Based Primer. The consensus among most project builders is that the best solution is to use an alcohol-based shellac sealer (B-I-N shellac primer/sealer). Take special note of the "shellac" component here. Other types of primer sealers, like water-base and oil-base sealers, just don't hold up against leaking resin from a knot.

This Works

The best solution for sealing stubborn knots in pine is to use an alcohol-based shellac sealer, like B-I-N shellac primer/sealer. Shellac works as an effective barrier between two chemical compounds—like the resin in a pine knot and the pigment in latex paint.

Doesn't Work

Most people mistakenly assume an oil-base primer will do the trick of sealing knots. Although these primers might appear to work at the start, the effect is short lived. Eventually resin from the knot will work its way through both a primer and a topcoat.

Doesn't Work

Unfortunately, water-base sealers are nearly useless in containing the resin that will continue to seep out of a pine knot. In fact, the sealer is likely to fail within just a few hours after brushing it on, as the resin quickly finds its way to the surface.

Clear Finish

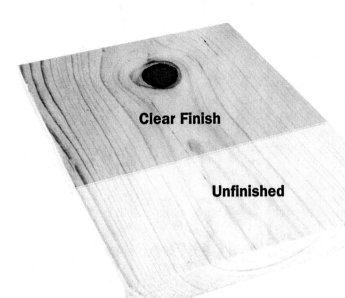

Clear Finish

Unfinished

Shopping for a clear finish can be confusing. Some are made with varnish, some with lacquer. Some are oil-base, some are acrylic—and that's not counting all the new hybrids. You'll have to decide for yourself which is best for your particular project, but hopefully my suggestions below can help guide you in the right direction.

The products I've listed on the following pages have worked really well for me, and I assuming they'll work reasonably well for you, too. If any of my choices seem odd, impractical, or unconventional by your standards, by all means go out and investigate the hundreds of other choices available!

Basic Steps for a Clear Finish

Prepare Wood
Starting with a smooth and clean board helps you avoid *big* finishing problems later on.

Apply Finish
First practice on a test board to see how your chosen finish behaves on wood.

Add More Coats
One coat of any finish is rarely enough. Be sure to lightly sand between each application.

Clear Finish: Step by Step

1

Start with Clean Wood

A shop vacuum will pick up 90 percent of dust left by sanding. Catch remaining dust by wiping everything down with a tack cloth.

2

Brush-On First Coat

When working with bare wood, I like to brush on the first coat (not wipe) to reach all the nooks and crannies in my project.

3

Let First Coat Dry

Check instructions on can to see how long to wait before applying a second coat. With most water-base finishes, it's about 2 hours.

My Top Choices for Clear Finish on Pine

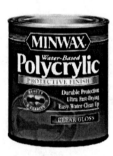

MinWax Poly

This is MinWax's most popular water-base finish. It's a nearly foolproof product that works on just about any kind of surface.

General Finishes

Rated *Best Brush-On* by *Fine Woodworking* magazine, this water-base clear coat has low VOCs *and* a low price.

Zinsser Shellac

Shellac is making a comeback of sorts in woodworking. It's good for wood—and good for the environment.

Kid Safe / Food Safe

Looking for a harmless finish? Fact is, regardless of the type of finish you apply, once it's completely dry, it can't really leak chemicals that might be ingested by a child or dinner guest. Keep in mind that I'm talking about a **completely cured** finish, which can take several weeks. Check the instructions on the can for specific drying and curing times.

Clear Finish: Step by Step

4 Sand First Coat

Sand with 220-grit paper to remove bubbles and brush strokes. Then wipe down again with a tack cloth to clean off the dust.

5 Wipe Second Coat

Use a cotton rag to wipe on a second coat. You might need to thin the finish to make it go on smoothly (see can for details).

6 Final Dry

Again, check the instructions on the can for specific drying times. For most water-base finishes, it's about 48 hours.

Brush or Wipe?

There's no right or wrong answer to this question. It's all about personal preference. As you've seen in my step-by-step instructions, I prefer to brush the first coat (to make sure I get into all the cracks), and then use a cloth to put on additional layers. This helps me get a super-smooth surface.

Staining Pine

Clear Coat

Stain (white)

Sealer

Staining pine can be tricky. Pine is notorious soaking up stain unevenly, which can leave stubborn blotches and streaks. Fortunately, there are a few preventative steps you can take to resolve the problem (see below). Keep in mind that stains add color, but they don't really protect the wood. That means you'll also need to apply a clear protective finish on top.

Water vs Oil

For simple wood projects made from pine, I prefer water-base stains over more toxic oil-base products. Water-base stains have a much lower VOC content, are available in more color choices, and are easy to clean up with soap and water.

Basic Steps for Staining Pine

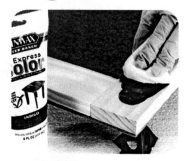

Conditioner
Start with a pre-stain conditioner to avoid blotches and streaks in your finished project.

Stain
Today you can choose from dozens of colors and shades, all available at your local home center.

Clear Top Coat
Best way to protect your completed project from dirt and scratches is to use a clear top coat.

Staining Pine: Step by Step

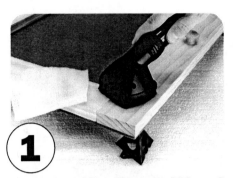

① Start with Clean Wood

Use a shop vacuum to pick up the bulk of dust left on your project. Catch the remaining dust by wiping everything down with a tack cloth.

② Apply Conditioner

Use a foam brush to reach all the corners and crannies in your project. Let the conditioner soak in for a couple minutes, then wipe off excess with a clean cloth.

③ Give it a Rest

With most water-base conditioners, you'll need to wait 15-30 minutes before moving on to the next step. Check the product can for specific instructions.

My Top 3 Choices for Pre-Stain Conditioners

Pre-Stain (water)

A water-base pre-stain is less toxic than its oil-base cousin (see right). Note: Be sure to use a water-base stain with this product.

Pre-Stain (oil)

If you plan to use oil-base stains, you'll have to use a compatible oil-base conditioner. MinWax Pre-Stain is ready to go out of the can.

SealCoat (shellac)

A woodworker's favorite! You'll need to thin it with denatured alcohol, though. Works with both water-base and oil-base stains.

Why Use a Conditioner?

Unfinished softwood, like pine and poplar, has a tendency to soak up stain unevenly. This can result in dark and light patches along the surface of a board, especially at the ends (end grain). A wood conditioner evens the playing field—preventing stain from settling too deep in some areas, too shallow in others.

Staining Pine: Step by Step

④ Light Sand—150 grit

The conditioner you applied in step 2 may have raised the grain slightly. Smooth it down now with 150 grit paper, then vacuum and dust the wood.

⑤ Apply Stain

Brush (or wipe) the stain in the direction of the grain, letting it penetrate for 1-2 minutes. Then remove the excess with a clean cloth (lightly dampened with stain).

⑥ Let Stain Dry

For most water-base stains, you'll need to allow at least 3 hours of drying time before applying a clear top coat. For oil-base stains, let it dry overnight.

My Top 3 Choices for Stain

Minwax Custom

Minwax has around 50 different color choices in water-base stains. These are custom-mixed at the counter (just like paint).

Minwax Wipe

This is by far the *easiest* and *quickest* way to get a stain finish on wood. Adding a clear top coat protects the stain.

General Finishes

For those who prefer to go the oil-base route, GF stains provide a high quality finish at a very reasonable price.

Brush or Wipe?

Your final project will probably look the same either way, but your choice of tools can make a big difference in how *messy* the job will be. Stain is thin, and will quickly drip and run from a cheap brush. Wiping with a cloth prevents most of that. A good fine-bristle brush will keep stain from running, but they're pricey.

Staining Pine: Step by Step

7
Apply Clear Top Coat
Apply a thin coat using a high-quality synthetic bristle brush. Apply in one direction with the grain. Be careful not to over brush, which can leave steaks.

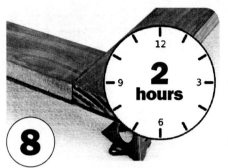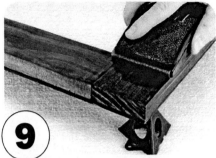

8
Let Clear Coat Dry
For water-base finishes, you'll need to wait about 2 hours before adding a second coat. For lacquer-based finishes, let it dry overnight (check label for details).

9
Sand Between Coats
I like to use 220-grit paper (or abrasive pad) between coats. If you're using water-base products, don't use steel wool (the trapped metal fibers will rust).

My Favorite Clear Coats (over stain)

Minwax Poly
This is Minwax's most popular water-base finish. It's a nearly foolproof finish that works on just about any kind of surface.

Minwax Spray
Sometimes it's just easier to spray a final topcoat. I won't do it in the house, though. It's outdoors with a mask for me.

Minwax Wipe-On
Easy-to-hold plastic container makes all the difference. Wipe it on with a cloth—no worry about drips or brush marks.

Stir, Don't Shake
You can shake paint cans as much as you like, but for clear finishes, stir only. Why? Shaking a clear finish creates bubbles in the can, which turn into small, hard bumps on your finished project. Gently stir finishes with a paint stick (grab several at your home center).

Painting Pine

One of the more practical choices for finishing pine is to simply paint the wood. Painting is somewhat less complex than applying stains. Plus, it's a job that most people are already familiar doing. However, this doesn't mean that painting wood is necessarily quick or easy. Getting a professional-looking paint job still takes a considerable amount of preparation—and patience. Follow along with me on the next few pages as I go through the process step by step.

Paint

Primer

The perfect paint job starts with a primer.

3 Basic Steps for Painting Pine

Clean Wood
Starting with a clean surface makes all the difference in getting a professional-quality paint job.

Apply Primer
Pine is difficult to cover with anything, especially paint. A primer is essential for getting good results.

Apply Paint
If you've done the right prep work, this step in the finishing process is like adding frosting to a cake!

Painting Pine: Step by Step

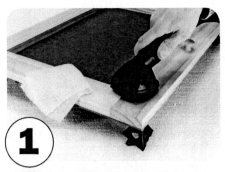

1 Start with Clean Wood

I like to use a shop vacuum to pick up any sanding dust left on a project. Then, as a final step, I quickly run a tack cloth over the surface to catch leftovers.

2 Apply Primer

Use a brush or foam pad to work the primer into all the corners, nooks and crannies. Don't worry about blotches, the final coat of paint will cover all that.

3 Let Primer Dry

Water-base primers usually require about 2 hours dry time before adding another coat. You can check your can label for specific drying times.

My Favorite Paint Primers

Zinsser B-I-N

It's hard to beat shellac-based primers for sealing stubborn resins in pine. Surprisingly enough, oil-base primers can't compete.

Zinsser BullsEye

As long as you're not trying to cover knots and resins, a water-base primer works fine on softwoods like pine.

Zinsser Zero

Although "zero" might be an exaggeration, the level of VOCs in this product is still considerable lower than most.

Why Primer?

Pine is a soft, porous wood that soaks up paint as fast as you can it brush it on. What's worse, the resins in softwood can continue to bleed through paint even after applying multiple coats. A good primer solves both problems. It provides a solid canvas for paint, and effectively seals pores, knots, and discolorations.

Painting Pine: Step by Step

4
Sand Primer
Use a 220-grit sandpaper to lightly smooth the surface of the primer coat. Then dust everything with a vacuum and tack cloth.

5
Apply Paint
To get a super-smooth surface, try using a small foam roller to apply your final coats of paint. Touch up edges with a small brush.

6
Dry Between Coats
Sometimes one coat is just not enough. With most water-base paints, wait at least 2 hours before applying another coat.

My Favorite Paint Choices for Pine

Rust-Oleum
Reasonably low VOCs, this paint is easy to find at home centers and hardware stores.

Olympic
Olympic is trying to make an environmentally-sound paint, and this one is getting there.

Sherwin Williams
Low VOCs and low odor makes this interior latex paint a good choice for wood projects.

Water vs Oil
Although some project builders still defend oil-base paints, I can't think of any good reason to use them—other than to cover the bottom of a boat. For most small wood projects, water-base paints do a perfectly good job of protecting wood, and in many cases, are better suited for projects than oil-base paints.

Painting Pine: Step by Step

7 Final Sand

I like to use a small rubber sanding pad with #220-grit paper to smooth over the final coat of paint. Go easy here—you just want to remove bumps, not the paint itself!

8 Apply Clear Coat

You can skip this step if you're already using a high-gloss paint to begin with. Otherwise, you'll need to add a clear finish to the final coat of paint for maximum durability.

9 Let Clear Coat Dry

Check your can label for specific drying times. In most cases, water-base products usually require 2 hours to dry. However, I like to wait overnight just to be safe.

My Top 3 Choices for Clear Coat over Paint

Polycrylic (brush)

Low VOCs and easy water clean up make this Minwax clear coat finish a favorite among wood project builders (that's me!).

Polycrylic (spray)

Sometimes spraying is just easier. Be sure to take safety precautions—like wearing a mask and working outdoors if possible.

Painter's Touch

I like this finish for its low VOCs, reasonable price, and easy soap-and-water clean up. It's easy to find at your local home center.

Milk Paint

Want to go all-natural? There's nothing more natural than milk paint. It's one of the oldest paint finishes around, dating back to the 16th century. Milk paint sold today hasn't changed much. It's still made with the same raw materials used 300 years ago—powdered milk protein and clay. No VOCs, no fungicides, no preservatives.

The best thing about milk paint is that it actually looks better as it gets older. Unlike typical paints that chip and peel, milk paint gently wears thin at the corners and edges, letting the underlying colors peek through. In fact, this kind of weathered look can be created intentionally (see layering and crackling below).

Get a Weathered Look with Milk Paint

Wash Coat

Create a country-style look to your project by applying thin layers of milk paint to unfinished wood. Milk paint has a translucent effect, which can look more like stain than conventional paint.

Layering

Easily create a weathered-and-worn look by applying multiple layers of milk paint—each in a different color. Once dry, lightly sand the edges to allow a hint of the underlying colors to show through.

Crackling

For the ultimate antique look, apply an "antique crackle" liquid between two coats of milk paint. The liquid causes the second coat to pull and break apart, much like paint does on antique furniture.

Test...Test...Test

Finishes can be unpredictable. That's why it's risky to brush it on the finished project without first testing it on a piece of scrap wood. Just make sure the scrap wood is the same type of board you are using on the actual project.

Milk Paint: Step by Step

① Start with Clean Wood

Use a shop vacuum to pick up remaining dust on your project. Then wipe everything down with a lightly dampened cloth.

② Conditioner (optional)

If you're concerned about blotching, try using a conditioner first to help the wood absorb milk paint more evenly.

③ Let it Rest

With most water-base conditioners, you'll need to wait about 15-30 minutes before moving on to the next step.

Paint   **Water**

1 : 1

I like to first mix the powder and water in a mason jar (a)—then pour just enough paint into a shallow bowl (b) to apply one coat.

Mixing Milk Paint

Milk paint comes in a powder that you'll have to mix with water. The basic ratio is easy: 1 part water to 1 part powder. However, this is only a suggestion. Feel free to experiment and find just the right opacity that suits your taste.

A simple paint stick works fine for mixing the powder. Don't put too much muscle into stirring, though. Milk paint has a tendency to foam up, which can leave a rough surface on your project boards.

Leftover Milk Paint—Although milk paint *powder* can last indefinitely (when stored in an air-tight container), after it's been mixed with water its shelf life is extremely short. Try to mix only enough milk paint for the day. If you end up with leftover paint, you're just as well to wash it down the drain than try to save it for another project.

Milk Paint: Step by Step

4

Apply First Coat

Use whatever you like to apply the paint—brush, roller, or pad. Don't worry if the paint seems streaky; this is natural for milk paint. Streaks can be covered with a second coat.

5

Let First Coat Dry

Milk paint feels dry to touch in about 30 minutes, but let the first coat dry a full two hours before doing any more work—like adding another coat or distressing the finish.

6

Sand First Coat

You'll like how easy it is to sand milk paint—it comes off in a light powder, leaving a nice smooth surface behind. Go easy, though. You can easily sand off too much paint.

EZ Clean Up

Milk paint is probably the easiest finish to clean up—simple soap and water does the job. Best part is that I feel much better about washing milk paint down the drain than a more toxic latex paint.

7 Apply Second Coat

Brush on the second coat just as you did the first (brush, roller, or pad). If you want to create a layering effect, use a different color milk paint for the second coat.

8 Let Second Coat Dry

Let the second coat dry a full two hours before doing any more work (like sanding or adding a top coat). Remember that milk paint *dries lighter* than it appears when wet.

9 Final Sanding

A final sanding brings milk paint to life with its deep, rich color. If you're creating the layering effect, lightly run your sanding block along the edges to reveal the first coat.

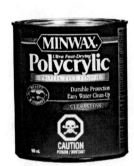

What About a Clear Top Coat?

Although not always necessary, applying a clear protective finish over milk paint might be a good idea for projects that need a more durable surface, like table tops and kids' furniture. Milk paint alone does not repel water, and will quickly spot from drips and spills. You can use any type of clear finish you like over milk paint, although I'd suggest finding a similarly eco-friendly product—like a low-VOC water based acrylic or a shellac.

Shellac

Shellac has lost much of its popularity over the years, but it's starting to see a slow comeback, especially with woodworkers wanting a more environmentally-friendly finish.

With a little research, you'll discover that shellac comes from an insect (can't get more natural than that). In fact, shellac is so natural it's approved by the FDA for use in food—like candy and vitamins. It's fast drying, offers great moisture resistance, and requires very little sanding between coats. What's more, the "de-waxed" variety makes a perfect wood sealer and base coat for any number of different finishes you might want to use as a final topcoat.

Shellac can be purchased ready-to-go out of a can, or in flakes, which you'll have to mix yourself with denatured alcohol. The only real danger in using shellac is that the alcohol content is extremely flammable. Fortunately, shellac dries fast, so the danger is short-lived.

Products Made with Shellac

Pre-Stain

Sometimes called a "wash coat" or "spit coat," shellac can be used as a conditioner to prepare wood for a stain. Most shellac-based conditioners are simply a full-bodied shellac that has been thinned and de-waxed.

Paint Primer

Shellac-based primers (like B-I-N) do a great job of preparing wood for paint. The natural sealing quality of shellac, combined with a white tint base, provides a solid foundation for creating a professional-quality finish.

Clear Finish

Shellac by itself can be an attractive, durable finish for wood projects. Shellac is available in a can, although some woodworkers prefer to make their own (raw shellac flakes mixed with denatured alcohol).

Latex
Acrylic
Copolymer
Waterborne
Petroleum
Enamel
Alkyds
Poly Acrylic
Polyurethane
Urethane
Silicone
Linseed
Soybean
Tung Oil
Cottonseed
Wax
Varnish
Shellac

Why So Many Finishes?

Understanding the differences between finishes can be tricky. For that I blame the labels, where terminology is often inaccurate to begin with (ie: latex paint does not contain latex). Try not to get too bogged down with the language, though. The best way to understand finishes is first divide them into two basic categories: water-base finishes and oil-base finishes.

Water-base Finishes

Just as the name implies, water-base finishes can be thinned and cleaned *with water*. Here are the most important advantages in using these water-base products:

- **Low VOCs** (volatile organic compounds)—better for you and the environment.
- **Quick drying time**—finish your project in one day.
- **Elasticity**—helps prevent cracking and peeling.
- **Color stability**—does not yellow over time.

Common Names for Water-base Finishes
- **Latex**—An old-fashioned name for acrylic (there is no latex in acrylic paint).
- **PolyAcrylic**—An acrylic finish composed of synthetic polymers.
- **Synthetic Polymers**—Filler-type resins used in acrylic finishes (vinyl and acetate).
- **100% Acrylic**—An acrylic finish with no synthetic polymers.

Oil-base Finishes

To be honest, I can't think of any good reason to use an oil-base finish, short of painting the underside of a boat. Today's water-base acrylics can do practically anything a traditional oil-base finish can do, and usually better. In fact, water-base products now use names taken from oil-base finishes—like water-base *polyurethane* and water-base *lacquer*—despite the fact that neither polyurethane or lacquer are actually used in these products.

Common Names for Oil-base Finishes
- **Polyurethane**—Clear varnish made from synthetic resins and oils.
- **Alkyd Enamel**—Hard surfaced, oil-base paint.
- **Linseed, Tung Oil**—Slow-drying oils used in varnishes and oil-base paints.

Two Interesting Alternatives

Two of my favorite finishes are *Shellac* (page 118)—an all-natural clear finish that dries fast and leaves no lingering VOCs after drying—and *Milk Paint* (page 114)—an all-natural paint powder that emits zero VOCs.

Toxicity in Finishes

As much as I like putting a nice finish on a wood project, that first whiff of fumes kind of spoils the experience for me. I suppose it's because I don't like getting bombarded with a witches' brew of chemicals the minute I open the can. Problem is, it's nearly impossible to finish a piece of wood without releasing some amount of toxins in the air.

Whether we like it or not, the chemical properties of a finish—the solvents, the pigments, and the binders—are what make a finish what it is. The trick is to choose a finish with the least amount of hazardous chemicals in the mix, but still effective in creating a durable surface. So what exactly makes one finish more hazardous than another?

Actually, it's a combination of different things, but the top three factors that really tell the story about how safe a particular finish might be are:

1) The VOC rating (see below)
2) The solvents used in the finish (see page 121)
3) How the finish is applied (see page 121)

Each of these play an important part in determining the overall toxicity of paints, stains, and clear finishes. It's important to consider **all three** factors before drawing any conclusions about how safe a finish really is.

VOC Rating

VOC stands for **volatile organic compounds**. Federal law requires that manufacturers include a VOC rating on the label. The rating is important because VOCs can pose certain hazards to the environment and to the person using the product. The rating is displayed in grams per liter (g/l), and tells us the relative concentration of VOCs that are present in the mix. As a general rule, the lower the VOC rating, the less potential hazard this product might pose. However, there's a little more to the story than that.

Is a Low VOC Rating Enough?

I think we can all be happy that manufacturers are developing new finishes with lower VOC ratings. That's the good news. The bad news is that we're often lead to believe that VOC ratings give a complete picture of the potential hazards lurking in the can. Unfortunately, this isn't always true. Sometimes understanding the true toxicity of a product goes beyond what a simple VOC rating can tell us. The VOC rating is not a complete picture of the toxicity of a finish, and that brings me to my second consideration when choosing a finish: **solvents** (see next page).

VOC ratings are listed on the back of can labels and on the MSDS data sheet (available online).

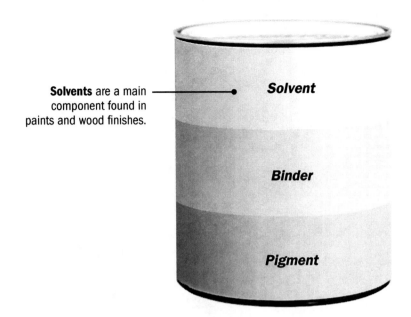

Solvents are a main component found in paints and wood finishes.

Solvent

Binder

Pigment

Solvents

There are a lot of different types of solvents used in finishes, but the most hazardous chemical solvents you should avoid in a finish are:

1. **Ethylene Glycol**
2. **Benzene**
3. **Toluene**
4. **Xylene**

These chemicals are linked to cancer, liver and kidney damage, and are even outlawed in some states. With all the new finishes that are out there today, there's really no reason for project builders like us to buy products that contain these chemicals.

Applying a Finish

Sometimes the best (and easiest) way to lessen the impact of hazardous chemicals is to simply be smarter about how you use the finish. Below are my favorite "rule-of-thumb" guidelines for working with finishes.

Buy What You Need

I know it's tempting to toss those near-empty cans of paint and stain into the trash, knowing very well the contents will ultimately leak into groundwater. Better to *buy only what you need* for the project at hand, and avoid leftovers entirely. If you do end up with leftovers, check with your local waste management office to find out about special pick-up days or drop-off points for getting rid of unused paint and finishes.

Work Outdoors

The best place to apply a finish is outside of the house—in a driveway, the backyard, or a detached garage with the door open. Of course this isn't always practical. So if you must work indoors, you'll just have to take a few extra precautions, like opening windows, running fans, and wearing a mask. If you're pregnant, have allergies, or are extra sensitive to chemicals, stay out of the area for at least 48 hours.

Use "Green" Finishes

In addition to the EPA's work in setting VOC guidelines, private groups have also taken up the cause—doing their own testing of paints and finishes and rating them accordingly. Look for low-VOC or zero-VOC products certified by groups like Greenguard, Green Seal, and the Master Painters Institute. Be prepared to spend more money on these products, as they are still relatively new to the market.

COMPARE VOC

WOOD CONDITIONERS

LOW VOC

VOC 40 g/l — Minwax Pre-Stain Wood Conditioner

VOC 239 g/l — General Finishes Pre-Stain

VOC 708 g/l — Minwax Pre-Stain Wood Conditioner

VOC 730 g/l — Zinsser Bulls Eye Seal Coat

VOC 755 g/l — Cabot Pre-Stain Wood Conditioner

HIGH VOC

WOOD STAINS

LOW VOC

VOC 81 g/l — Minwax White Wash Pickling Stain

VOC 94 g/l — Minwax Color Clear-Tint Base

VOC 135 g/l — Minwax Express Color

VOC 240 g/l — General Finishes Wood Stain

VOC 525 g/l — Minwax Gel Stain Wood Stain

HIGH VOC

PAINT PRIMERS

LOW VOC

VOC 0 g/l — Bulls Eye Zero™ Primer

VOC 100 g/l — Zinsser Bulls Eye 1-2-3 Primer

VOC 350 g/l — Benjamin Moore Fresh Start®

VOC 450 g/l — Zinsser Cover Stain Primer

VOC 550 g/l — Zinsser BIN Shellac-Base

HIGH VOC

PAINT

LOW VOC

VOC 0 g/l — Old Fashioned Milk Paint

VOC 50 g/l — Benjamin Moore Ben Acrylic

VOC 180 g/l — Rust-Oleum Painter's Touch

VOC 375 g/l — Benjamin Moore Impervo® Enamel

VOC 487 g/l — Rust-Oleum Marine Topcoat

HIGH VOC

What's in a Clear Finish?

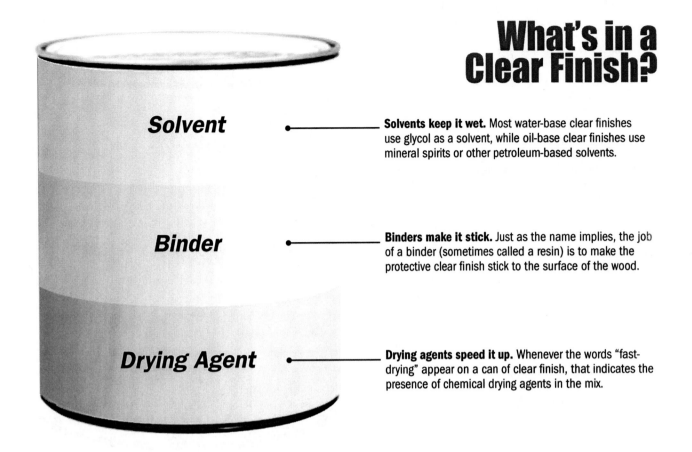

Solvent

Solvents keep it wet. Most water-base clear finishes use glycol as a solvent, while oil-base clear finishes use mineral spirits or other petroleum-based solvents.

Binder

Binders make it stick. Just as the name implies, the job of a binder (sometimes called a resin) is to make the protective clear finish stick to the surface of the wood.

Drying Agent

Drying agents speed it up. Whenever the words "fast-drying" appear on a can of clear finish, that indicates the presence of chemical drying agents in the mix.

VOC Levels in Common Clear Finishes

HIGH VOC	VOC 621 g/l	VOC 575 g/l	VOC 440 g/l	VOC 103 g/l	VOC 54 g/l	LOW VOC

Minwax® Gloss Clear Lacquer

General Finishes Arm-R-Seal

Minwax Polyurethane

MinWax PolyCrylic

Rust-Oleum Painter's Touch

What's in a Can of Stain?

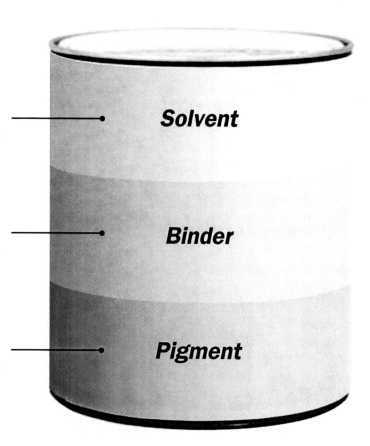

Solvents keep it wet (while it's in the can). Once stain is applied to wood, the solvents evaporate and leave the binder and pigment behind. Water-base stains typically use glycol ether as a solvent, while oil-base stains use petroleum-based solvents like mineral spirits.

Solvent

Binders make it stick. The job of a binder (sometimes called resin) is to make the color (pigment) in stain stick to the surface of wood. Binders in water-base stains are typically made of acrylic resins, while oil-base stains use alkyds and natural oils.

Binder

Pigments give color. When applied to wood, pigments penetrate the fibers and permanently stain the wood with whatever color you have chosen.

Pigment

VOC Levels in Common Wood Stains

HIGH VOC	VOC 525 g/l	VOC 240 g/l	VOC 135 g/l	VOC 94 g/l	VOC 81 g/l	LOW VOC
	Minwax® Gel Stain	General Finishes® Wood Stain	Minwax® Express Color	Minwax® Wood Stain	Minwax® Pickling Stain	

What's in a Can of Paint?

Solvent

Solvents keep it wet. The primary job of a solvent is to keep paint from drying while it's in the can (and keep it wet while it's still on your brush).

Binder

Binders make it stick. The job of a binder (sometimes called resin) is to make color (pigment) stick to the surface of the wood.

Pigment

Pigments give color. Most paints contain base-coat of white pigment (titanium dioxide) that you'll need to have tinted at the counter.

Thickener

Thickener adds body. Some paints include a chalky substance that adds body and thickness to the paint. (Don't worry, it's nontoxic.)

Fungicide

Fungicides fight mold. Some paints include chemicals (like formaldehyde) to inhibit mold and bacteria.

VOC Levels in Common Paints

HIGH VOC	VOC 487 g/l	VOC 375 g/l	VOC 180 g/l	VOC 50 g/l	VOC 0 g/l	LOW VOC
	Rust-Oleum Marine Topside®	Benjamin Moore Impervo® Enamel	Rust-Oleum Painter's Touch®	Benjamin Moore Ben® Acrylic	Milk Paint Old Fashioned®	

how to build anything
Extras

Shop guides & templates for making your next wood project easier (and more fun) to build.

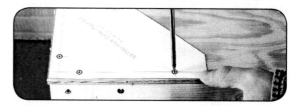

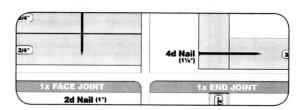

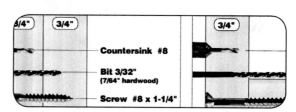

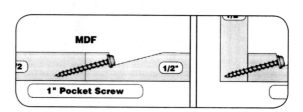

Plywood Cutting Guide

Step-by-step instructions for building a cutting
guide custom-fitted to your circular saw.

Build a Plywood Cutting Guide

One of the best ways to cut plywood is to use a circular saw. However, you'll need some type of guide to help you cut a straight line. You can buy a *manufactured* cutting guide for several hundred dollars—or build your own for less than $20.

No More Guessing

The big advantage with this cutting guide is that it automatically aligns your blade to cut precisely against the cut line, without having to peer over, under, or around your saw to see if the blade is hitting its mark.

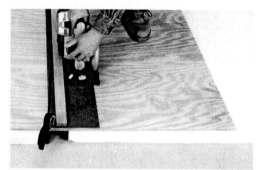

What You'll Need: Materials & Tools

Hardboard
Start with a half sheet of 1/8" thick hardboard.

Fence
Buy the straightest piece of 1x2 oak or maple you can find (min. 48")

Clamps
You'll need four hand clamps to build the guide.

Circular Saw
The guide is designed to be custom-fitted to your saw.

Glue
Wood glue keeps the fence permanently fixed.

Anatomy: Plywood Cutting Guide

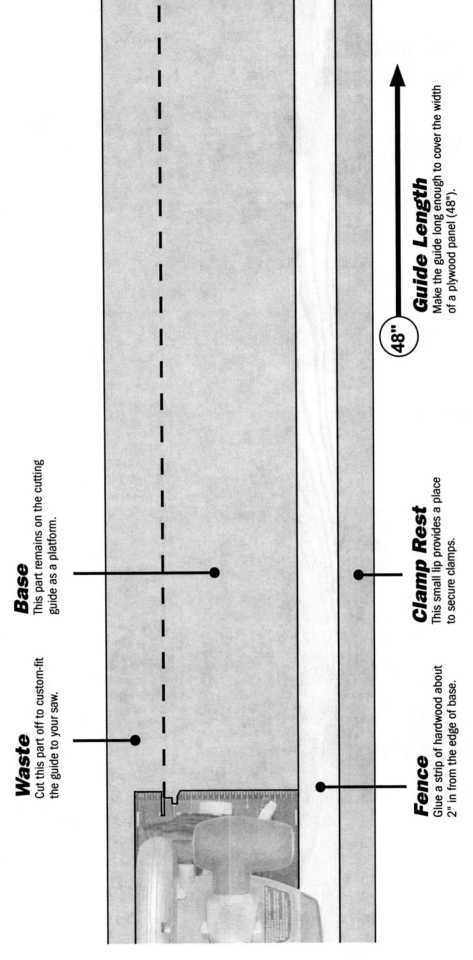

Waste
Cut this part off to custom-fit the guide to your saw.

Base
This part remains on the cutting guide as a platform.

Clamp Rest
This small lip provides a place to secure clamps.

Fence
Glue a strip of hardwood about 2" in from the edge of base.

48"

Guide Length
Make the guide long enough to cover the width of a plywood panel (48").

How to Build
Plywood Cutting Guide

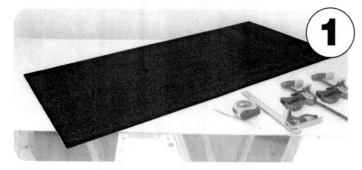

Start with the Base

The material for the base doesn't need to be fancy—something like 1/8" hardboard works fine. If you don't already have some in the shop, go ahead and buy a 4' x 4' hardboard sheet at your home center. The 4' width will match up nicely with the 4' fence you'll be making below. Later you will trim the base to fit your saw, but for now make the base roughly 18" x 48"

Find a Straight Fence

I made my fence from a piece of hardwood molding, found at my local home center. Look for something that is made of oak or maple and is at least 48" long. Because this is the board that will guide your saw, it needs to be as straight and square as possible (see page 25). Check it by placing the board against something you already know is flat—like a granite counter top or a large glass window.

Glue Fence to Base

Glue and clamp the fence to the base. Place the fence roughly 2" away from the edge. This will give you a place to attach clamps later on. Apply a thin coat of glue to the underside of the fence and clamp it down securely. Be sure to clean up any glue that has squeezed out. Let this dry overnight before moving on to the next step.

(WASTE)

Trim Base to Fit Saw

This part is easy—just line up your saw against the fence and cut away whatever extra baseboard is sticking out beyond your blade. As you can see in the photo, I clamped the guide down to a couple of sawhorses before I started making the cut.

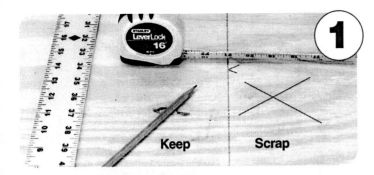

Mark Your Cut Line

1 Pull a tape measure from one side of the panel and mark where the cut should be located. Do this in three different places to make sure you've measured accurately. Then "connect the dots" with a straight edge (a drywall square works nice). Be sure to mark which side to keep—and which side to scrap.

Line Up the Guide

2 Place the panel cutting guide up flush against the cut line you just drew. Be sure to place the guide on the *keep* side of the cut line—keeping in mind that the edge of the guide marks the outer edge of your project piece.

Clamp it Down

3 Make sure your cutting guide is clamped down securely before starting the cut. The 2" lip on the back of the guide provides a nice spot for applying clamps (see photo). Keep in mind that when cutting a 4-foot wide panel, you'll only be able to use two clamps—one at each end of the guide.

Start Cutting!

4 Once everything is lined up and clamped down securely, the next step should be a snap. Start your saw at one end of the panel, applying moderate pressure against the fence as you push forward. When you reach the end of the cut, be sure to let the blade come to a complete stop before moving it away.

How to Use
2 Easy Methods

1. On the Floor with Styrofoam

Plywood panels are so big and awkward that sometimes it's just easier to cut them on the floor. Of course you'll need some way to keep the saw blade from hitting the concrete underneath—and that's where Styrofoam comes in.

Look for Styrofoam sheets in the building supplies section at your local home center. Ask them to cut a 4x8 sheet in half for you (makes it easier to get home). Lay the two sections on the floor, with a gap in the middle to allow space for your saw blade and clamps.

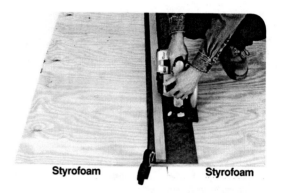

Styrofoam   **Styrofoam**

2. On Sawhorses

Sometimes I just don't have enough floor space to use the Styrofoam method shown above. Instead I'll use a pair wood sawhorses to create a vertical cutting station—similar to the panel saw you might see at a home center. A 1x4 strip attached to the bottom of each sawhorse creates a small lip on which to rest the panel.

No doubt this method takes a little more skill and courage for the average DIY builder to tackle. But with some careful planning, a good supply of wood clamps, and little patience, this method might be a better approach to cutting panels than crawling around on your knees in the garage.

A Note About Safety

Using a circular saw in this position can be more dangerous than cutting panels on the floor. The saw could potentially strike your body, if it were to go astray while holding it up off the floor like this. That's why it's extremely important to take the following precautions:

1. If this method feels uncomfortable...don't use it.
2. Make sure all pieces are securely clamped down.
3. Make sure your blade guard is working properly.
4. If the saw resists moving, stop and release trigger.
5. Let blade come to complete stop before pulling away.

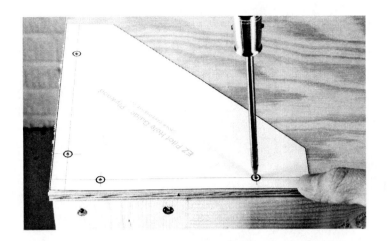

how to build anything
Pilot Hole Guides

No more guessing! Get perfectly aligned
pilot holes on every board.

 **BOOK CUTOUT**

Pages marked with this symbol
are designed to be cut from this
book for use in the shop.

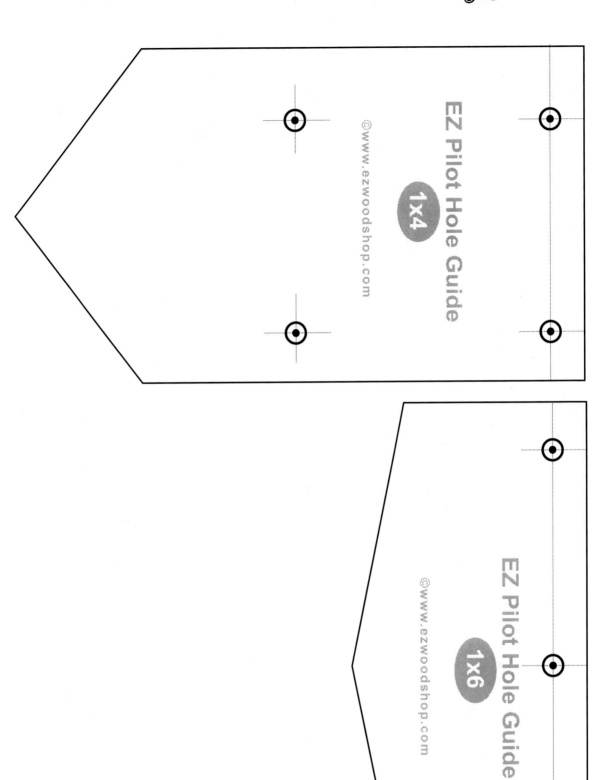

EZ Pilot Hole Guide

1x4

©www.ezwoodshop.com

EZ Pilot Hole Guide

1x6

©www.ezwoodshop.com

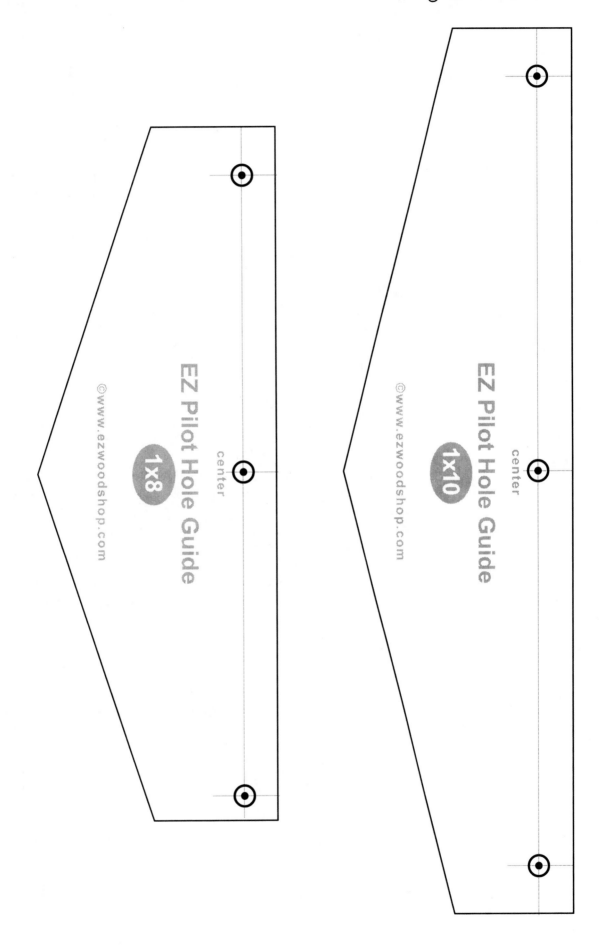

EZ Pilot Hole Guide

1x8

center

©www.ezwoodshop.com

EZ Pilot Hole Guide

1x10

center

©www.ezwoodshop.com

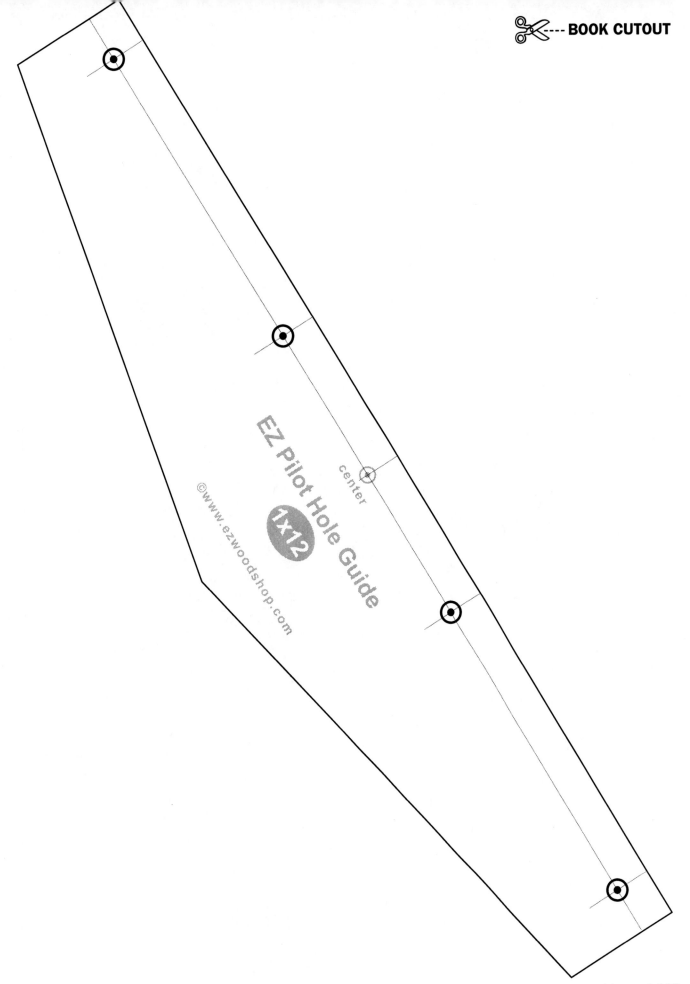

EZ Pilot Hole Guide

1x12

center

©www.ezwoodshop.com

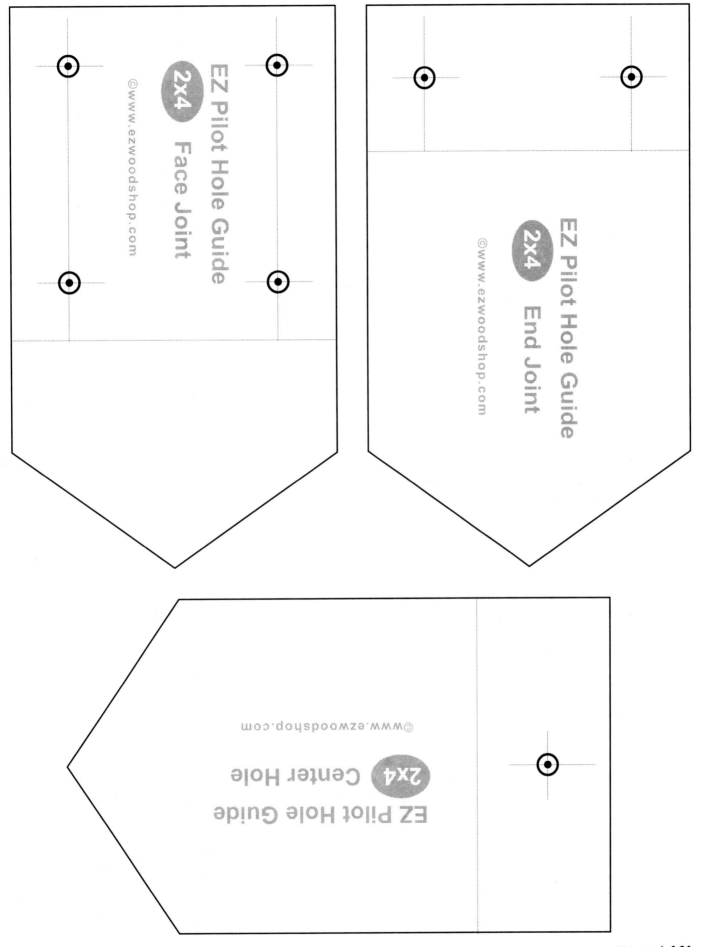

EZ Pilot Hole Guide
2x4
Face Joint
©www.ezwoodshop.com

EZ Pilot Hole Guide
2x4
End Joint
©www.ezwoodshop.com

EZ Pilot Hole Guide
2x4
Center Hole
©www.ezwoodshop.com

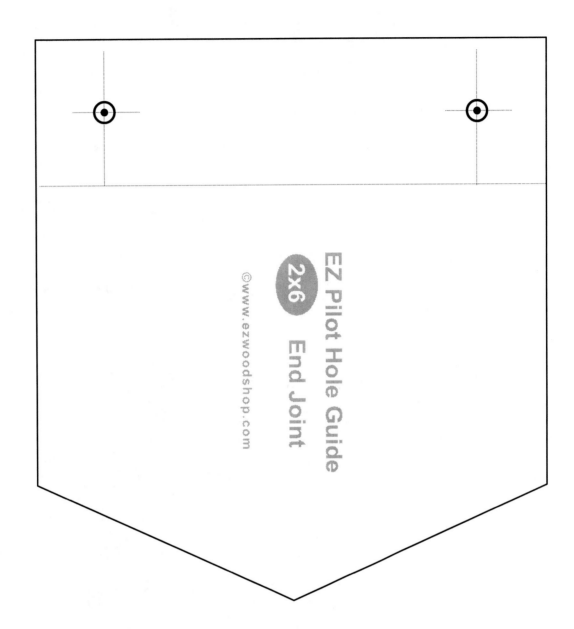

EZ Pilot Hole Guide

2x6

End Joint

©www.ezwoodshop.com

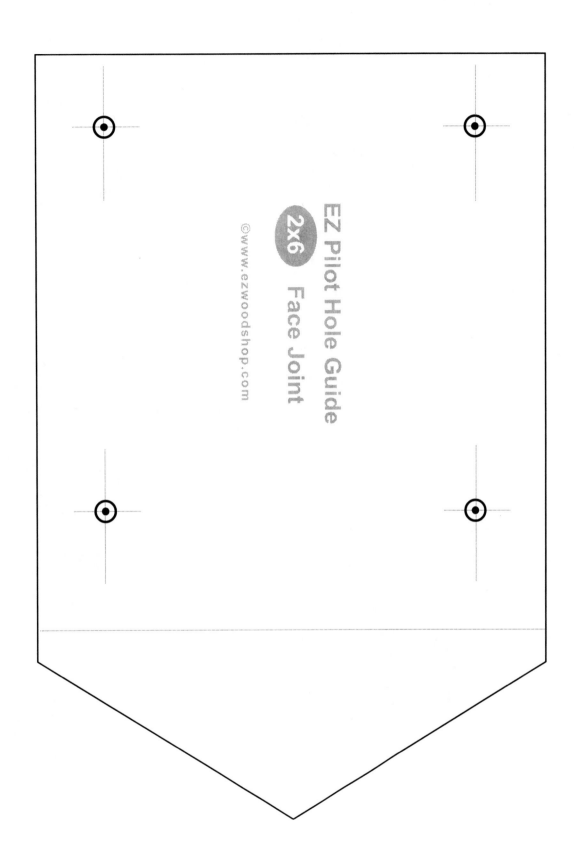

EZ Pilot Hole Guide

2x6 Face Joint

©www.ezwoodshop.com

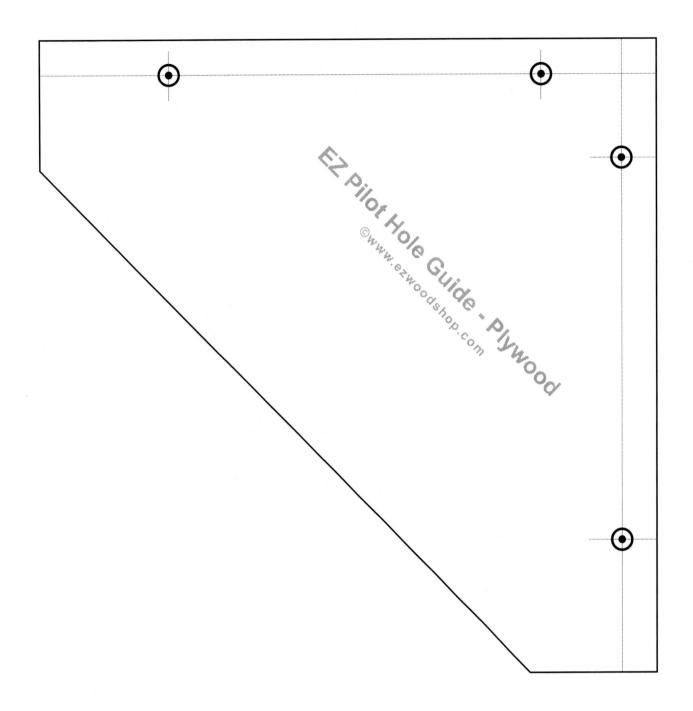

EZ Match: Nail Joinery

✂---- BOOK CUTOUT

1x FACE JOINT

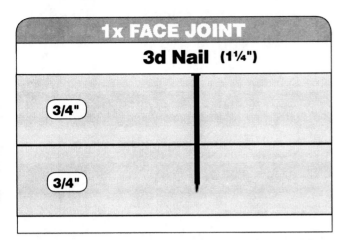

3d Nail (1¼")

3/4"

3/4"

1x END JOINT

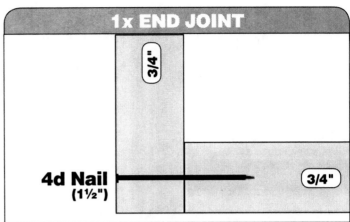

3/4"

4d Nail (1½")

3/4"

1x FACE JOINT

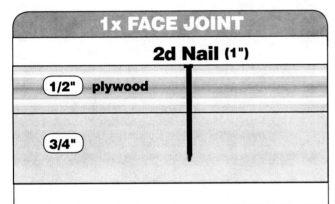

2d Nail (1")

1/2" plywood

3/4"

1x END JOINT

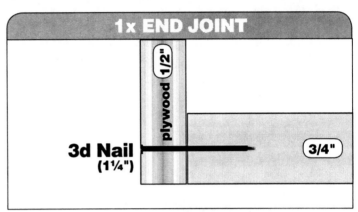

1/2" plywood

3d Nail (1¼")

3/4"

2x FACE JOINT

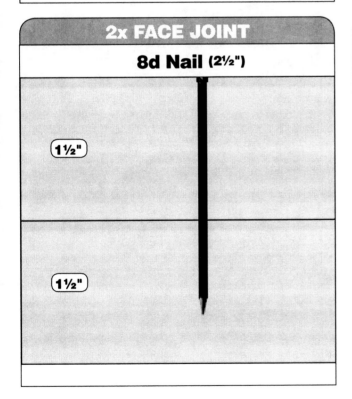

8d Nail (2½")

1½"

1½"

2x END JOINT

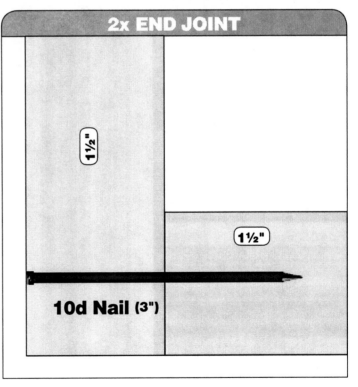

1½"

1½"

10d Nail (3")

EZ Match: Bit & Screw

 **BOOK CUTOUT**

1x FACE JOINT

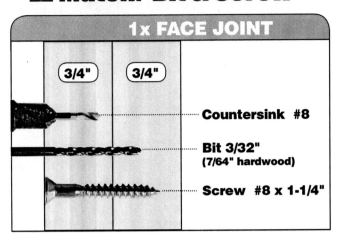

3/4" **3/4"**

Countersink #8

Bit 3/32"
(7/64" hardwood)

Screw #8 x 1-1/4"

1x END JOINT

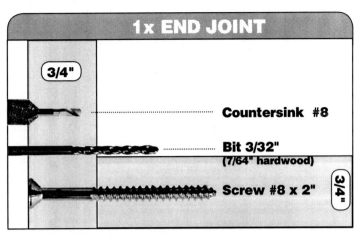

3/4"

Countersink #8

Bit 3/32"
(7/64" hardwood)

Screw #8 x 2"

3/4"

(1x FACE JOINT 1/2")

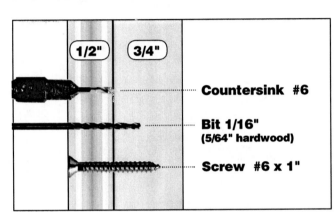

1/2" **3/4"**

Countersink #6

Bit 1/16"
(5/64" hardwood)

Screw #6 x 1"

(1x END JOINT 1/2")

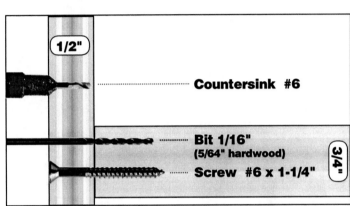

1/2"

Countersink #6

Bit 1/16"
(5/64" hardwood)

Screw #6 x 1-1/4"

3/4"

(1x FACE JOINT 1/4")

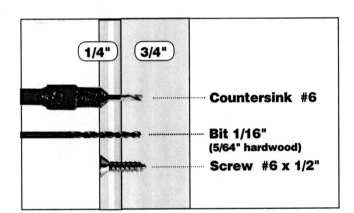

1/4" **3/4"**

Countersink #6

Bit 1/16"
(5/64" hardwood)

Screw #6 x 1/2"

(1x END JOINT 1/4")

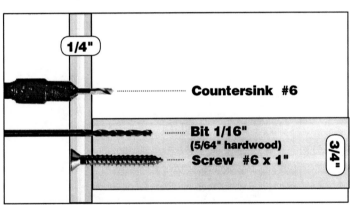

1/4"

Countersink #6

Bit 1/16"
(5/64" hardwood)

Screw #6 x 1"

3/4"

2x FACE JOINT

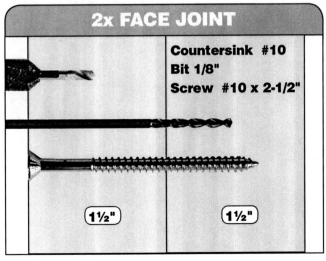

Countersink #10
Bit 1/8"
Screw #10 x 2-1/2"

1½" **1½"**

2x END JOINT

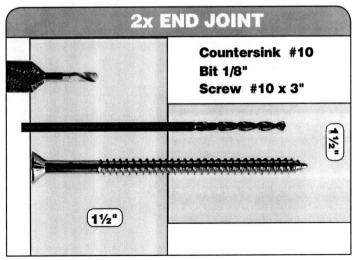

Countersink #10
Bit 1/8"
Screw #10 x 3"

1½"

1½"

EZ Match: Pocket Hole Screws

 **✂----- BOOK CUTOUT**

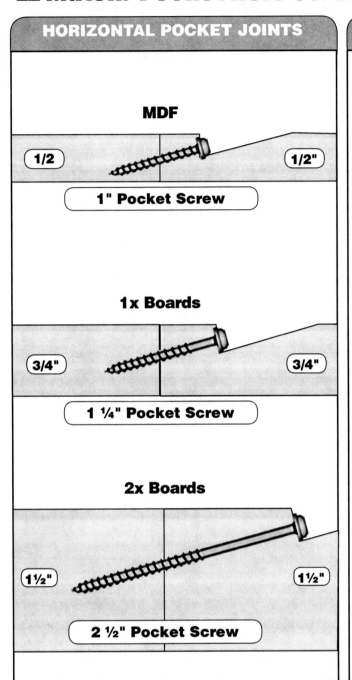

HORIZONTAL POCKET JOINTS

MDF

1/2 · 1/2"

1" Pocket Screw

1x Boards

3/4" · 3/4"

1 ¼" Pocket Screw

2x Boards

1½" · 1½"

2 ½" Pocket Screw

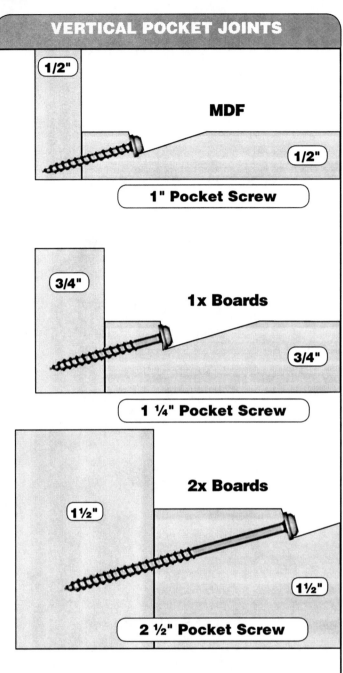

VERTICAL POCKET JOINTS

1/2"

MDF

1/2"

1" Pocket Screw

3/4"

1x Boards

3/4"

1 ¼" Pocket Screw

1½"

2x Boards

1½"

2 ½" Pocket Screw

Pocket Screw Chart (all sizes)

Board	Screw Size	Board	Screw Size
1/2" (13mm)	1" (25mm)	1-1/8" (29mm)	1-1/2" (38mm)
5/8" (16mm)	1" (25mm)	1-1/4" (32mm)	2" (51mm)
3/4" (19mm)	1-1/4" (32mm)	1-3/8" (35mm)	2" (51mm)
7/8" (22mm)	1-1/2" (38mm)	1-1/2" (38mm)	2-1/2" (64mm)
1" (25mm)	1-1/2" (38mm)		

Coarse or Fine?

Use coarse-thread pocket hole screws with softwoods—like pine and plywood. Use fine-thread screws with hardwoods—like oak, maple, walnut, and cherry.

Coarse Thread—Softwood

Fine Thread—Hardwood

CPSIA information can be obtained at www.ICGtesting.com
Printed in the USA
BVOW06s1847030314

346534BV00009B/175/P

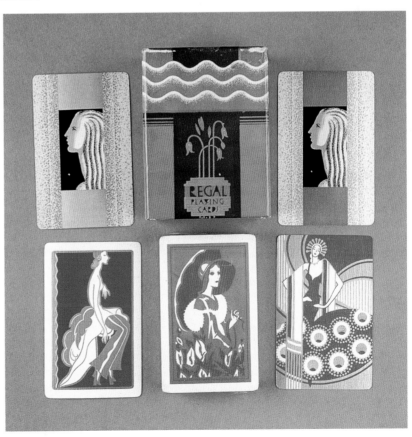

Above:
Nine decks with beautiful Deco ladies. Top row: left, USPC; center, Vivienne Diana cards by Gibson Art Company; right, "Ranee," artist: Gray Donna, Bicycle. Middle row: left, Hamilton; center, "Promenade," Congress, USPC; right, USPC. Bottom row: left, "Elaine" Diana cards by Gibson Art Company; center, "Butterfly," USPC; right, Hamilton. $15-25 each.

Above right:
Nine decks with lovely Deco ladies. Top row: left, Gibson Art Company; center, L.G. Sloan's Ltd, England; right, Boulevard. Middle row: left and center, Arrow. Bottom row: left and right, Belmar Criterion; center, Hamilton. $15-25 each.

Right:
More lovely ladies. Top row: double deck and box. George Allen, Inc. Regal Playing Card Company. Bottom row: left, Russell Playing Cards. Right, Arrow. $35-75 each.

Above:
Double deck of cards. Artist: Helen
Mckie. John Waddington, England. Rare.

Above left:
Left, Alf Cooke made for Woolworth's,
England. Right, "Clouds of the West."
Thomas de La Rue. England. $10-25 each.
Top: box for "Clouds of the West."

Left:
Twelve Deco decks. Top row: left,
Hamilton and Russell; right, Hamilton and
"La Russe," Russell. Middle row: Left,
"Fantasy," USPC and Hamilton. Right,
"Papillon," USPC and Russell. Bottom
row: left, "Pamfilo," Congress and French
Line by Catel & Farcy, Paris; right, 1939
World's Fair and "Pamfilo," Congress.
$20-50 each.

Bridge set in leather case with pencil. Rapid Tally Score Card, 1936. Double deck of cards. International Card Company. Canada. $50-75.

Six Deco decks of cards. Top row: left and center, Congress. Bottom row: left and right, Congress. Top right and bottom center: unmarked. $15-25 each.

Six Deco decks of cards. Top row: left, Bicycle-USPC; center, Park Avenue Playing Card Company; right, unmarked. Bottom row: left, Diana Cards by Gibson Art Company; center, USPC; right, Bicycle-USPC. $15-25 each.

Two round decks of cards. Arrow Playing Card Company. $25-40 each.

Deck of cards. Bid-Rite. $10-20.

Top left: unmarked. All others: The New York Consolidated Card Company. $25-40

Left, playing cards. Hotel Presidente, Habana.
Right, Large fan bridge tally. $15-40 each.

The bridge craze brought about bridge sets, bridge tallies, and place cards with great Art Deco graphics. Many of these were published by The Buzza Company, Gibson Art Company, and Rust Craft. Beautiful women were often the subjects.

Greeting card catalog. 1929. The Buzza Company.

Two pages from the Buzza catalog.

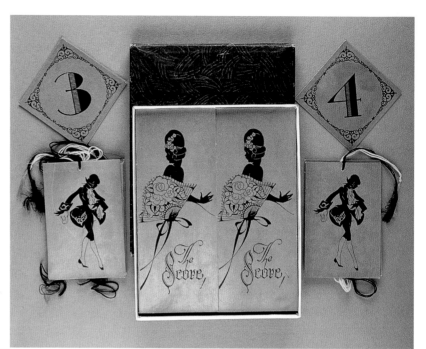

Bridge set. Four pads, sixteen tallies and four table numbers. Colonial Art, Inc., Minneapolis. 1926. $50-85.

The Colleen bridge set. Three pads and twelve tallies. The Buzza Company. $45-80.

Inside of "The Colleen" set.

Left, Gold bridge pad and four tallies. Right, "Finesse" set. Gibson Art Company. Four pads and sixteen tallies. The pads and tallies are "Dolores" and "The Belle." There are matching playing cards available. $40-65 each.

Seventeen piece bridge ensemble. Two pads, eight tallies and product brochure advertising beauty products for young women. 1931. The Colgate Company. $45-75.

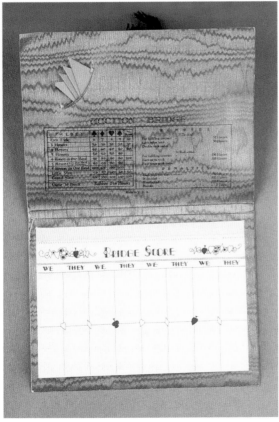

Inside of the gold set.

Two bridge sets from the 1933 Chicago World's Fair. Each has two pads and eight tallies. C.A. Brewer & Sons, Chicago. $50-100 each.

"Travel Bridge Set." The Buzza Company. $50-90.

Two pads and eight tallies from travel set.

Cover of "Nouvelle" bridge set. Four pads and sixteen tallies. The Henderson Line, Cincinnati. $50-80.

"The Hollywood" bridge set. Two pads and eight tallies. Buzza-Cardoza, Hollywood. $45-65.

Whist score cards and box with pencils. Left and center, "Crazy Whist." The Dainty Series. Right, "New Novel" Whist. The Dainty Series. England $35-50 each.

Tallies and bridge pads from the "Nouvelle" set. The parrots on the bridge pads are trump indicators. The original set also had a bon bon container and a pencil holder, which are missing.

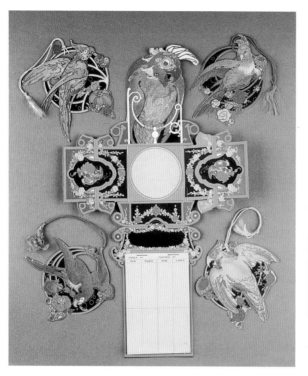

"It's The Vogue" Bridge Set. Four pads and sixteen tallies. The Buzza Company. $40-90.

Decorative bridge set. Four pads and sixteen tallies. Gibson Art Company. $40-70.

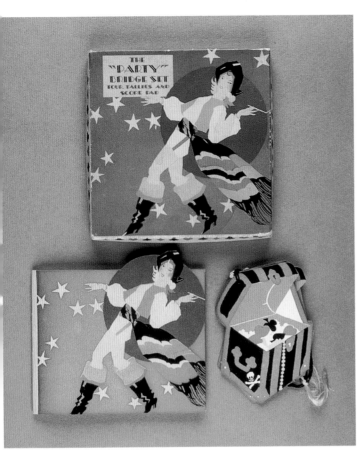

"The Party" Bridge Set. One pad and four tallies. $25-45.

"Bridal Bridge Ensemble." Four pads and sixteen tallies. The Buzza Company. $35-85.

Bridge score pad. Gibson Art Company. $8-15.

Three bridge pads. Top two, The Buzza Company. Bottom, Gibson Art Company. $5-12 each.

Bridge pad and matching box. The Henderson Line. $20-35.

Three bridge pads. Left, The Buzza Company. Right, both Avondale. $5-14 each.

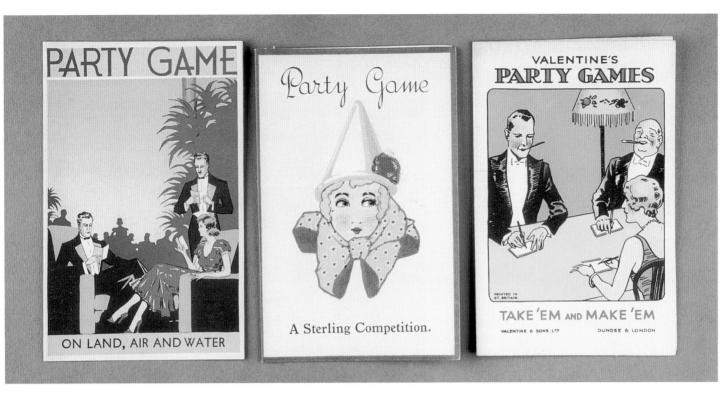

Three party game cards. These were word association games that had great Art Deco graphics on the cards and the box. England.

Four sample card bridge tallies. USPC. $8-15 each.

Large bridge tally of lady with a heart-shaped banjo. Gibson Art Company Art. $10-15.

Back of lady with banjo bridge tally.

Four lady bridge tallies. Top left, The Henderson Line. All others, Rust Craft. $8-20 each.

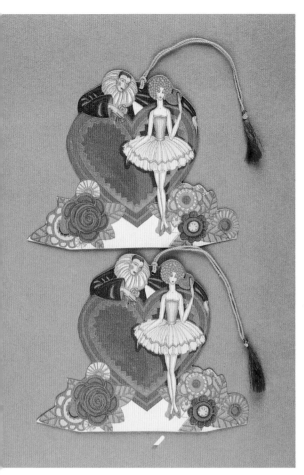

Two bridge tallies. Hallmark. $8-20 each.

Three lady bridge tallies. $5-15 each.

Tally

Table No. 1 7   Couple No.
2 8
3 9
Date 4 10   Total
5 11
6 12
Name

Four lovely Deco lady bridge tallies. Top left, unmarked. Bottom left, The Buzza Company. Top and bottom right, The Henderson Line. $8-20 each.

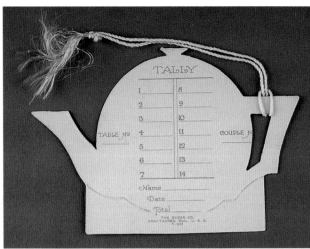

The back of Buzza tally.

Two bridge tallies. The Buzza Company. $8-15 each.

Wedding bridge tallies. Top row, all by Gibson Art Company. Bottom row, left, The Henderson Line; center, The Buzza Company; right, unmarked. $8-20 each.

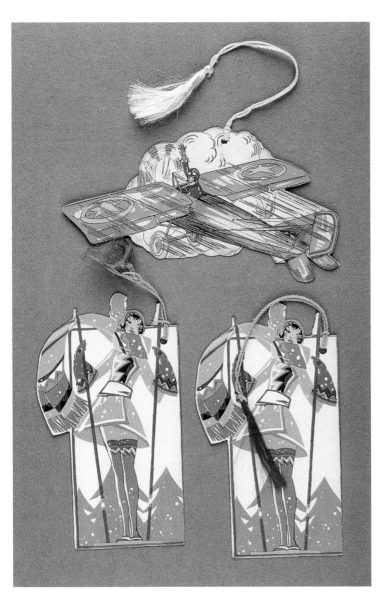

Large shamrock bridge tally. The Buzza Company. $8-18.

Three bridge tallies. Top, Hallmark.
Bottom, The Buzza Company. $8-20 each.

Three St. Patrick's Day bridge tallies. All
by the Buzza Company. $8-18 each.

Large Christmas bridge tally. $8-18.

Two New Year's bridge tallies. Gibson Art Company. $8-18 each.

Two Halloween bridge tallies. The Buzza Company. $10-20 each.

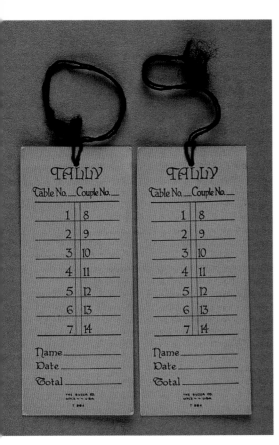

The backs of Halloween tallies.

Four Christmas bridge tallies. Charles S. Clark , Company. $8-15 each.

Halloween bridge tally. The Buzza Company. $10-20.   Back of Halloween tally.

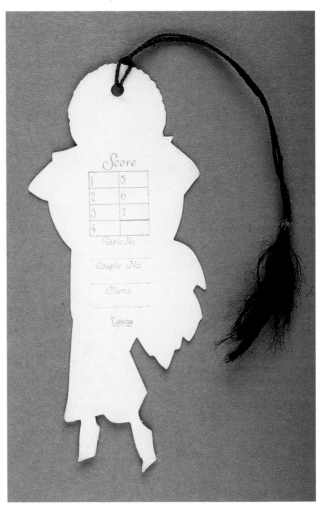

Large bridge tally. Gibson Art Company. $8-18.

Two fan tallies. Top, The Buzza Company.
Bottom tally has pencil attached. $5-16 each.

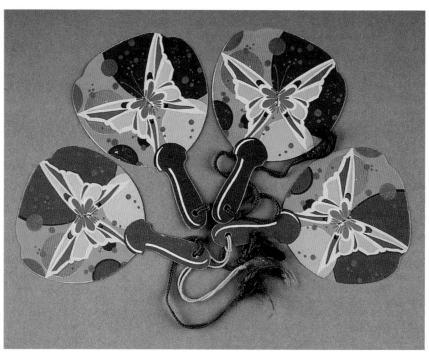

Small fan bridge tallies. The
Buzza Company. $5-15 each.

Large stick fan tally. $8-20.

Stick fan tally. $10-20

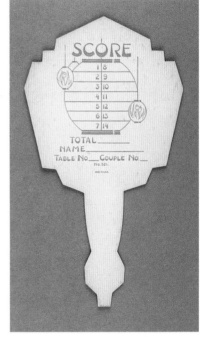

The back of stick fan tally.

Four small fan tallies with flowers.
The Buzza Company. $5-15 each.

Small stick fan tally. $8-15.

Four lady bridge tallies. Hallmark. $8-15 each.

Three square tallies. All by the
Buzza Company. $8-18 each.

Three square lady tallies. Bottom left, The Buzza
Company. Others, unmarked. $8-18 each.

Four uncut bridge tallies. Zoric Garment
Cleaning System. 1931. $35-50 each.

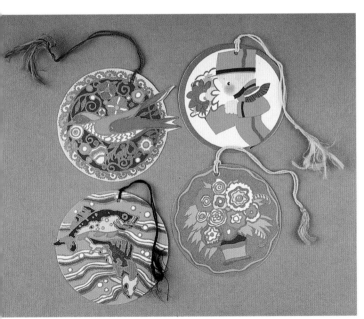

Four round bridge tallies. All by the Buzza Company. $8-15 each.

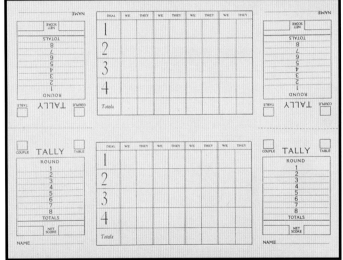

Back of Zoric tally.

Left and right, decorative bridge table numbers.
The Henderson Line. Center, bridge table cover
pins and box. $45-75 each.

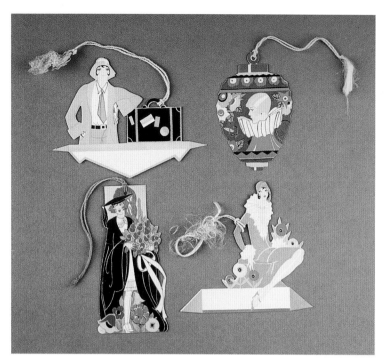

Four lady bridge tallies. Top left, Gibson Art Company. Top right, Charles S. Clark Company. Bottom left, The Henderson Line. Bottom right, Gibson Art Company. $8-18 each.

Four lady place cards. All by the Buzza Company. $8-15 each.

Four lady place cards. Top and bottom, Charles S. Clark Company. Center two, Gibson Art Company. $8-15 each.

Four lady place cards. Top right, Quality Park. All others, The Buzza Company. $8-15 each.

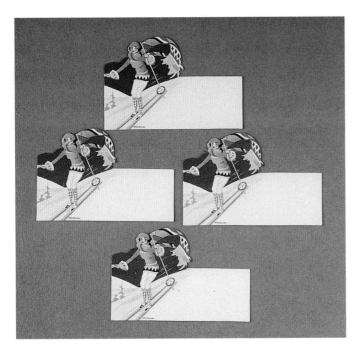

Four lady skier place cards. Dennison. $8-15 each.

Three New Year's place cards. Top two, P. F. Volland Company. Bottom, the Buzza Company. $8-18 each.

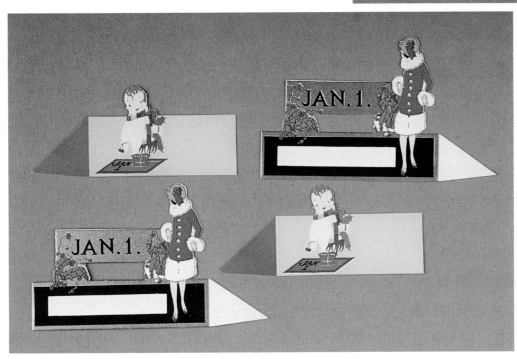

Four New Year's place cards. Top left and bottom right, Gibson Art Company. Others, unmarked. $8-12 each.

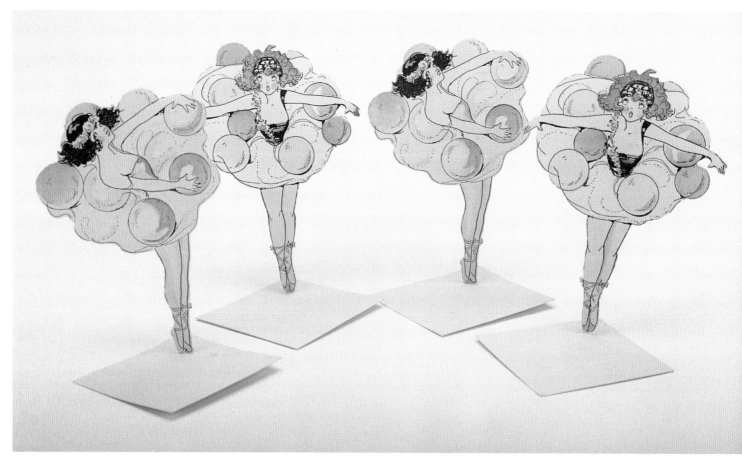

Four mechanical stand-up place cards. $10-20 each.

Four mechanical stand-up place cards. $10-20 each.

Eight mechanical stand-up place cards. Kimball by Charles S. Clark Company. $10-20 each.

Four mechanical stand-up place cards. Left and third, the Buzza Company. Others, unmarked. $10-20 each.

Place card. Artist: Veldy. France. $10-20.

Three place cards with men. All by the Buzza Company. $8-18 each.

Three lady place cards. Top and right, the Buzza Company. Bottom left, Charles S. Clark Company. $8-18 each.

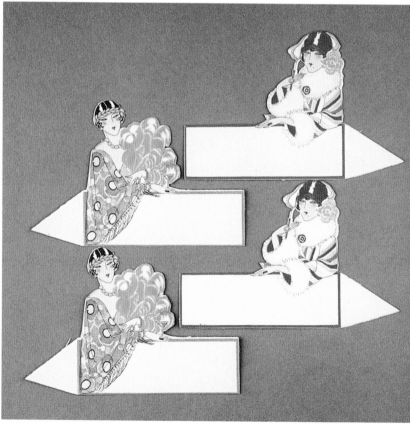

Four lady place cards. $8-12 each.

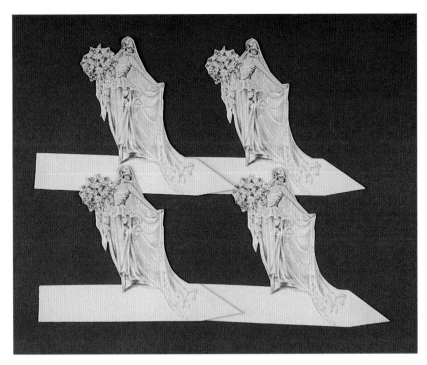

Four bridal place cards. $8-18 each.

Four paper coasters. $1-5 each.

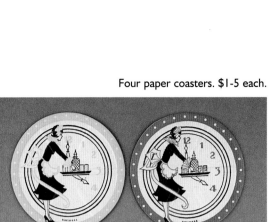

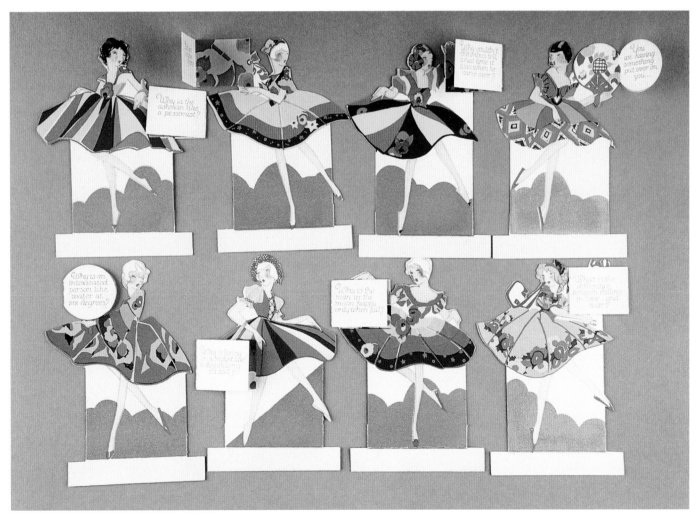

Place card set. Eight place cards by P. F. Volland Company. $8-18.

Decorative fan. $25-50.

During the art deco era, many game manufacturers hired artists to make their boxes and contents appealing to children and the adults who purchased them.

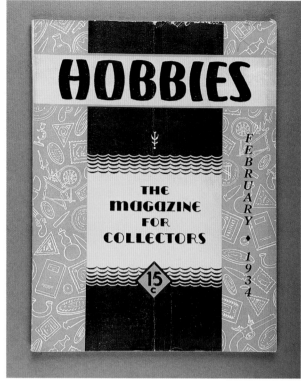

Magazine cover. *Hobbies*. 1934. $10-20.

Two boxes of badminton shuttlecocks. Left, National Products Sales Corp, Boston. Right, R.S.L., England. $25-50 each.

"Kick-Back" pinball game. Joseph Schneider, Inc. New York. $75-125.

Rainbow Dominoes. Hal-Sam. $10-25.

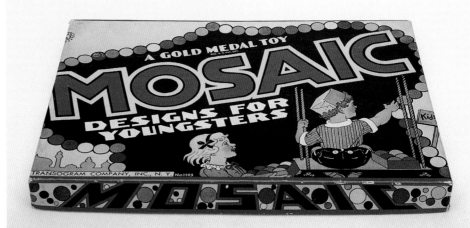

"Mosaic" game. Transogram Company. Inc. 1935. $20-40.

"Picture Weaving," Samuel Gabriel & Sons. $35-50.

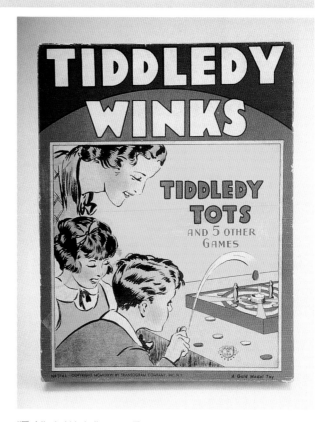

"Tiddledy Winks" game. Transogram Company. Inc. 1937. $20-45.

Two games. Left, "Bingo." Milton Bradley. $20-25. Right, "Chance-Road," metal gambling game. France. $175-250.

Catalog cover. *Hobby Craft Treasure Chest of Toy Designs*. Artist: F. Ephares. 1937. $25-35.

Chapter 2
Advertising and Packaging

The commercial and graphic artist became an integral part of advertising in the 1920s. Advances in reproducing art and the improved quality of the reproductions added to the rising trend. The use of wood engraving, photography, color, and line illustrations by magazines and newspapers, using some of the best artists of the time, made commercial art a new and growing field. In the United States, the use of the art director for popular magazines like *Saturday Evening Post* and *Vanity Fair* raised the level of creativity in publicity.

The 1930s saw a blossoming of trademarks and product name recognition. Everything from the hood ornaments of automobiles to soap labels had a look that told the consumer what company it represented. The advertising and the packaging, no matter what the product, were geared toward fantasy. The advertiser's goal was to make the consumer believe that a man who was successful would drive a certain car or wear a suit by a certain manufacturer. But women were to become the real target market. In the 1930s, smoking became acceptable for women, which begat a plethora of ads to make smoking look glamorous and sexy. The ads for soaps and detergents showed smiling, happy housewives doing the laundry and dishes. American advertising artists, using color and vibrant graphics in magazine ads, made everyday items, like baking soda, hairpins, and motor oil, look appealing.

The rise in modern typography and the use of the best artists for advertising led to the development of trade societies, whose aim was to ensure that quality was of the highest standard and the most modern of the time. In 1914 the American Institute of Graphic Arts was founded, followed in 1920 by the Art Directors Club in New York City. In England, the Society of Industrial Artists and Designers was founded in 1930. This later became the Chartered Society of Designers.

Before the 1920s, the public relied on point-of-purchase displays on store counters to see the new products. With the advent of modern publicity, the companies had to be more creative and competitive. New packaging went hand-in-hand with modern advertising. Packaging with Art Deco graphics was featured at the Paris Exposition of 1925. Box wrappers, labels, and container shapes were in a constant state of change, always trying to more effectively catch the consumer's eye. Product identification was becoming more important and the graphics used were sometimes the most important thing about the product. Anything could be dressed up in vibrant, Deco graphics and made to look like it was better than the competitor's product. The cosmetic industry was one of the largest proponents of using Art Deco graphics to differenti-

ate products that were virtually the same, such as lipstick and face powder. To this day packaging is one of the main reasons that this industry is so successful.

Advertisers were advised that because of the immediacy with which the public responds to the visual and written ad, streamlining is just as useful in advertising as it was in automobiles and other modes of transportation.

The tobacco and liquor industries were at the forefront in using graphics to sell their products. With the lifting of Prohibition and women smoking, these two industries took off and packaging was of the utmost importance. Kodak used the famous industrial designer, Walter Dorwin Teague to design its distinctive packaging. He designed cameras and packaging for Kodak for 30 years starting in 1927.

This is a category that is very abundant and easy to find today. Prices vary according to condition, how common an object is, and if it is artist signed. Paper shows, flea markets, garage sales and especially old house sales are great places to find the advertising and packaging items.

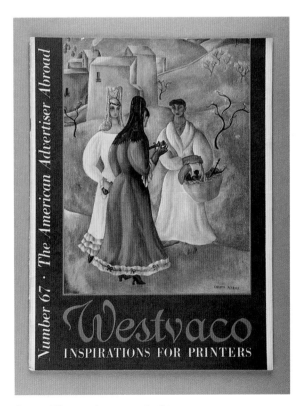

Cover. *Westvaco Inspiration for Printers*
Number 67. Artist: Carlotta Petrina.

Advertising sample for the West Virginia Pulp and Paper
Company in *Westvaco* Number 29. Artist: Jean Dupas.

Here are some fine examples of the use of Art Deco
graphics to dress up the candy industry.

Catalog cover. Austin Davis Company. 1932. England. $35-65.

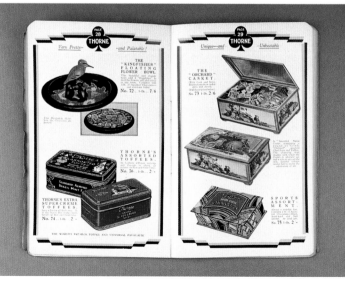

Illustration from the Austin Davis catalog.

Top left, Ultra Pak candy tin. Page & Shaw. New York. Bottom left, candy tin for Hotel New Yorker. Center, package for Penthouse Coffee. Pittsburgh. Right, coffee tin for Sto-Mike Coffee Company, Ltd. England. $25-65 each.

Three candy boxes. Left, Boston Confectionary Company. Center, Lovell & Covel. Right, Daggetts. All Boston. $35-85 each.

Holiday candy tin. Mrs. Southern. New York. $15-50.

Candy tin. $15-50.

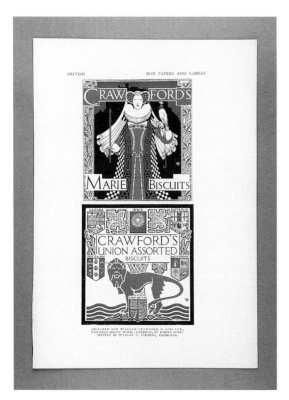

Box paper and label samples for Crawford
Biscuits, Edinburgh. Artist: Robert Burns.
Published in *Art and Publicity*. 1925. London.

Candy box hand-painted on gold foil.
Lovell & Covel. Boston. $45-85.

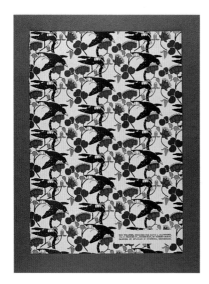

Box wrapper sample for
Crawford Biscuits, Edinburgh.
Artist: Robert Burns. Published in
Art and Publicity. 1925. London.

Cookie tin. DeMet's. Chicago. $35-75.

Side of tin.

Three candy tins. England. $15-75 each.

Candy box for Maple Grove Park salt water taffy. $20-45.

Candy box. Cella's. New York. $15-30.

Left, Confectioner ad. 1923. Paris. Right, Brusson Jeune weight reducing product pamphlet. Artist: Gaillard. France. $5-25 each.

Six tins. Left back: C.W.S. Biscuits; center, Betta Biscuits; front, C.W.S. Biscuits. Right back: Maison Lyons Petit Fours; center, Canco; front, C.W.S. All mentioned are made in England. $25-75 each.

Brochure for Jurasin Macon raisins. France. $15-25.

Mechanical display for Jaffa oranges and grapefruits. Artist in the style of Tom Purvis. Belgium. $50-75.

The 1920s and 1930s, during and after Prohibition, were the beginnings of the billion dollar tobacco and liquor advertising industry. The beautifully designed and illustrated advertising fans were used mostly in the liquor, fashion, and cosmetic industries.

Left, metal cigarette holder. Right, musical decanter. The decanter is stamped Japan, therefore it is probably post World War II. $75-125 each.

Lucky Strike ad. 1929.

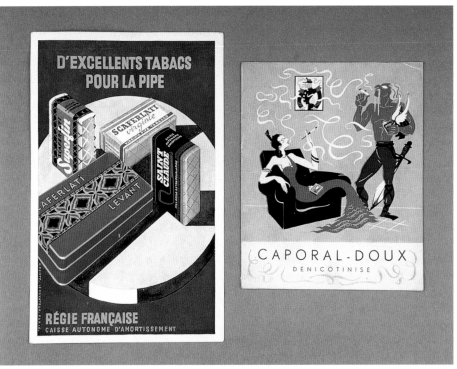

Two tobacco ads. Left, Régie Française. Artist: M. Ponty. Right, Caporal-Doux pamphlet. Artist: André Giroux. France. $15-25 each.

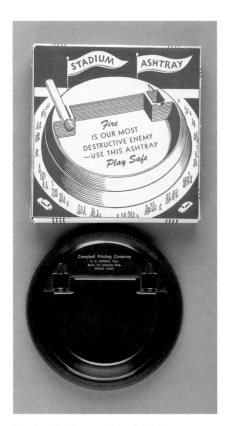

"Stadium" ashtray in box. $25-45.

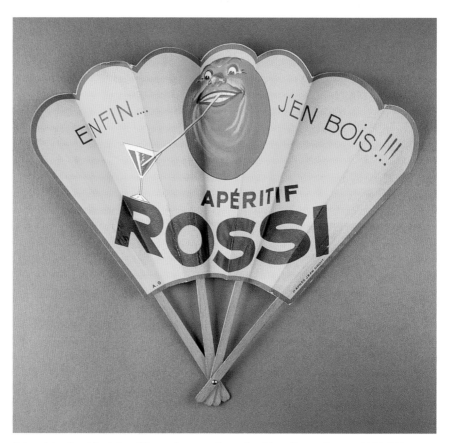

Advertising fan. Martini and Rossi. Artist in the style of Jean Droit. France. $100-300.

Left:
Cardboard stand up display sign. Alfa cigarette papers, with attached pack of papers. Artist: Hamerycky. France. $50-75.

Tobacco catalog. Artist: René Vincent. 1933. France. $25-50.

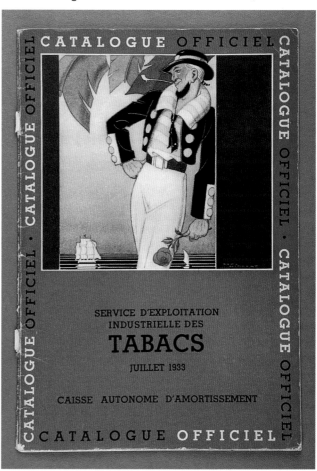

Two advertising fans. Left, Romano Vermouth, artist in the style of DE Ram. Right, Amourette liquor, artist in the style of EM Rahuél. Paris. $35-75 each.

Advertising fan. Marie Brizard liquors. Artist: J. Ganne. France. $100-300.

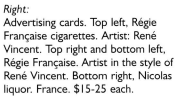

Right:
Advertising cards. Top left, Régie Française cigarettes. Artist: René Vincent. Top right and bottom left, Régie Française. Artist in the style of René Vincent. Bottom right, Nicolas liquor. France. $15-25 each.

Cigarette ad for Régie Française. Artist: A. Moluggon in the style of Henry Le Mommier. 1932. *femina* magazine. France.

Two wine labels. Left: unsigned. Right, artist: Leonetto Cappiello. France. $25-75 each.

LektroLite flameless cigarette lighter in box. 1945. $15-35.

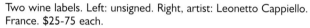

Advertising fan. Perrier-Jouet. Paris. $100-350.

Two food labels. France. $10-20 each.

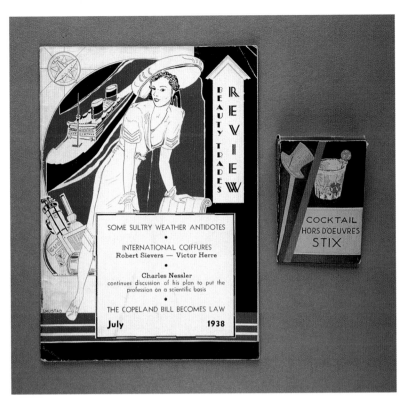

Left, *Beauty Trades* catalog. 1938. Right, Lewis Line cocktail sticks. $15-45 each.

Below:
Left, binoculars and box. Quick-Sight. Center, Etna Spill Maker. Both England Right,"Art Glo" enamel paint can. U.S.A. $15-45 each.

Here are some diverse examples of the use of Art Deco graphics in advertising.

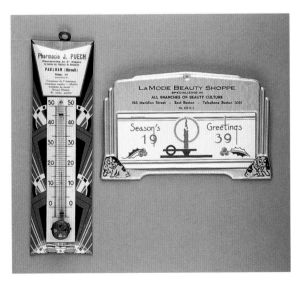

Advertising card. Landon's Cleaners. Watertown, New York. $10-25.

Left:
Left, a wall thermometer for Pharmacie J. Peuch. France. Right, a metal desk calendar for La Mode Beauty Shoppe. 1939. Boston. $15-30 each.

Blotter book. The Mirror Steam Laundry Co. 1935. Putney, England. $15-25.

Left, Marcelette wave maker set. Right, Wildroot Wave Set. $15-35 each.

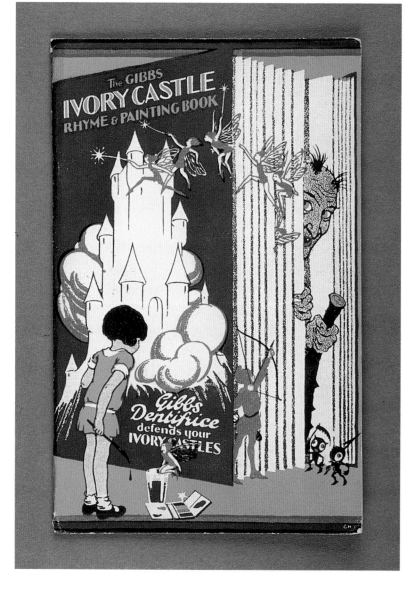

Coloring book for Gibbs Dentifrice. England. $10-30.

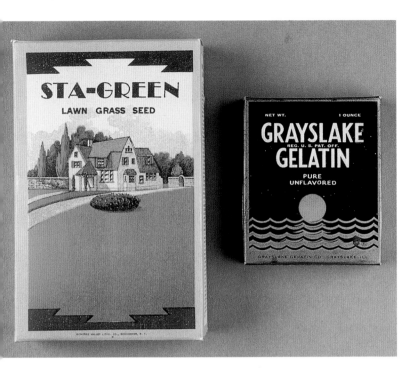

Left, Sta-Green grass seed. Right, Grayslake gelatin. $20-45 each.

Cardboard store display sign. Grimoz sanitary napkins. France. $35-75.

Store display. Perfect razor blades. Elsmere Cutlery Company, New York. $50-100.

Showcard sample for Vigil Silk Company, England. Artist: S.S. Longley.

Cardboard stand up display sign. Jak Tar disinfectant. England. $45-85.

Left, blotter for the Stetson Hat Company. Right, game booklet for Pertussin Cough medicine. $15-25 each.

Soap label. France. $25-50.

Catalog for Duoflux floodlights. The Benjamin
Electric Company. 1934. London $10-20.

Advertising banner. Ever Ready
batteries. England. $50-75.

Christmas banner. Ever
Ready. England. $50-75.

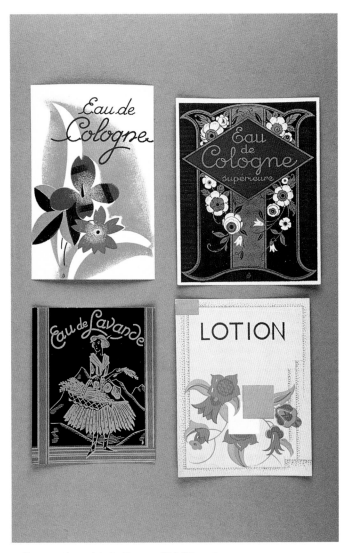

Four perfume labels. France. $10-25 each.

Four perfume labels. France. $10-25 each.

Four perfume labels. France. $10-25 each.

Canvas and metal products catalog. The Hettrick Manufacturing Company. Toledo, Ohio. $35-65.

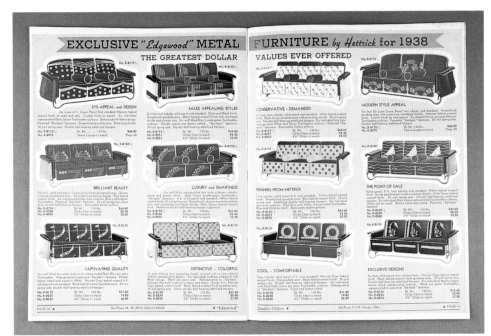

Illustration from the Hettrick catalog.

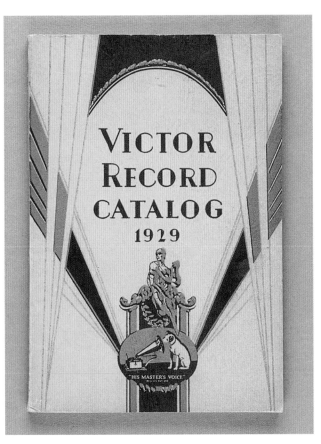

Catalog for the Victor Talking Machine
Company. 1929. New Jersey. $10-20.

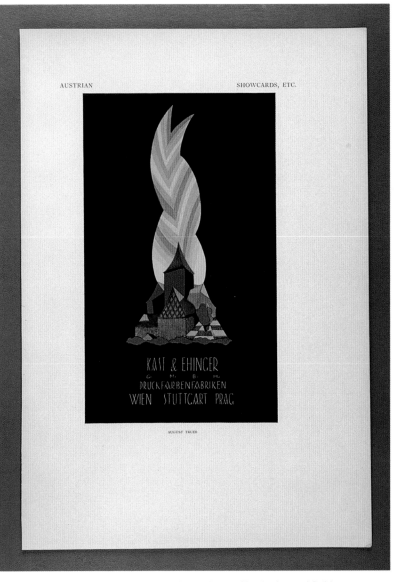

Showcard for Kast & Ehinger. Austria. Artist: August Trueb. Art and Publicity.

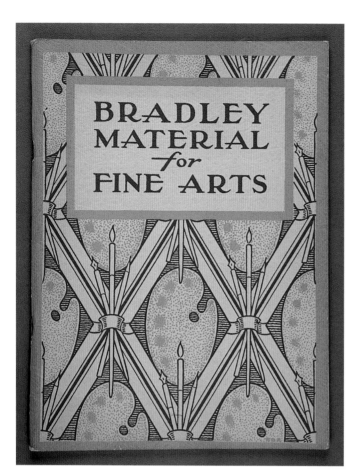

Catalog cover. Milton Bradley Company. 1938. $25-50.

Cover. Milton Bradley Idea Booklet. 1930. $15-35.

Cover. Milton Bradley Idea Booklet. 1930. $15-35.

Illustration from Milton Bradley Idea Book.

Back, Pere Cygne dye chart. Front, La Lorraine clothing dye. France. $45-65.

Left, Waterman's Ink and box. Center, Parker Ink. Right, Stafford's Ink and box. $15-30 each.

Pelikan ink blotter. Germany. $20-35.

Cardboard sign. Ox-Line Paint Company. $10-20.

Advertisement for Lange. Original watercolor, artist: Rachel Muirhead. 1930. $200-300.

Advertising sign. Filver suspenders and accessories. France. $25-75.

The geometric box designs by Walter Dorwin Teague for Kodak.

Chicago Evening Post ad. 1928.

Three cameras in boxes. All Kodak, designed by Walter Dorwin Teague. $10-100 each.

Two cameras with boxes. Both Falcon, made by Utility Manufacturing Company, $25-75 each.

Stand up display ad for Bibendum the Michelin Tire Company trademark man. France. $35-50.

Streamlined style used in automobile advertising.

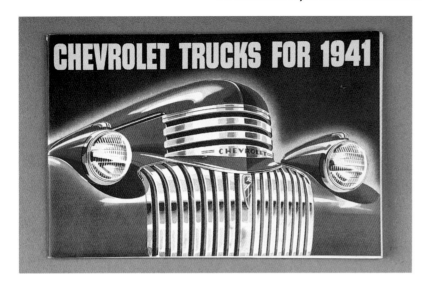

Catalog for 1941 Chevrolet trucks. $25-55.

Catalog for 1936 Oldsmobile. $25-75.

Illustration of 1937 Oldsmobile.

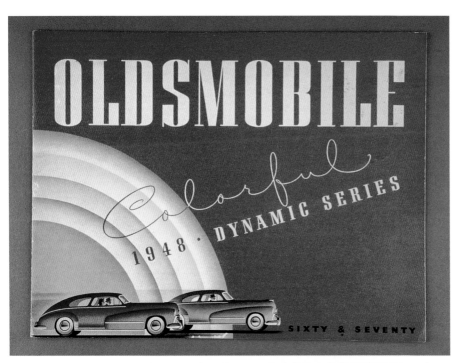

Catalog for 1948 Oldsmobile. $25-75.

Brochure of 1936 Lincoln Zephyr. $25-55.

Brochure for 1935 Dodge Commercial cars. $25-45.

Some wonderful examples of the use of Art Deco graphics for box and box wrappers.

Catalog for Seward Trunk and Bags. 1937-38. $35-65.

Gift box. Lipkins furniture store. Easton, Pa. $45-75.

Inside of Lipkins box showing baby bottles. The middle one is a bank.

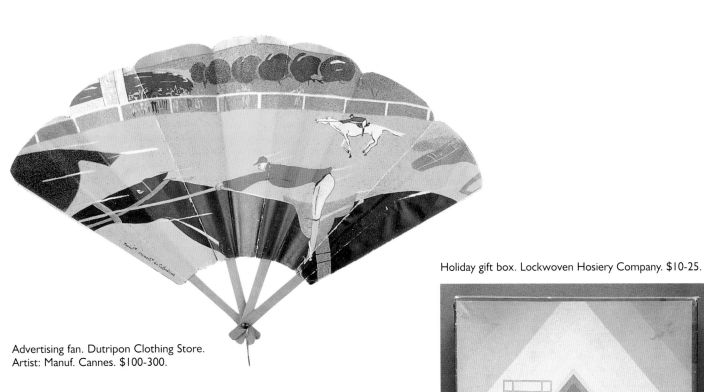

Advertising fan. Dutripon Clothing Store.
Artist: Manuf. Cannes. $100-300.

Holiday gift box. Lockwoven Hosiery Company. $10-25.

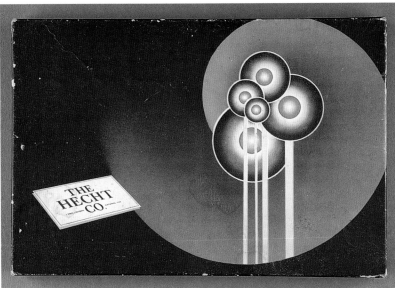

Gift box. The Hecht Company. $10-20.

Six assorted holiday gift and
candy boxes. $15-40 each.

Box for Turkish towel set. $10-25.

Advertising box label. Batger's Christmas Crackers. England. $20-45.

Inside of box of Tom Smith Christmas Crackers. England. $50-75.

Large holiday gift box. $25-45.

Tom Smith Christmas Crackers. England. $50-75.

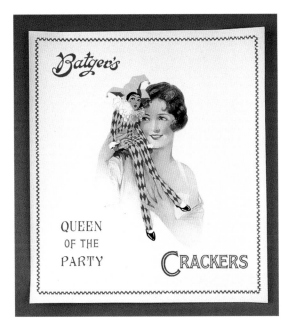

Advertising box label. Batger's
Christmas Crackers, artist: Leslie Fllig.
$20-45.

Advertising box label. Batger's
Christmas crackers. England. $20-50.

Chapter 3
Household

In the late 1920s and early 1930s, Depression green was the color of the kitchen and most of the dishes. With the introduction of streamlined, modern design, and the use of Art Deco graphics, the kitchen was transformed into a cheery, white, bright, and colorful place for the housewife to be happy. Industrial designers like Raymond Loewy and Norman Bel Geddes turned their attention to designing refrigerators and other small and large appliances for the home. Appliance companies put out booklets and brochures with interesting and attractive graphics on the covers. Paper clothing patterns were developed allowing any woman with a sewing machine and a little talent the possibility of dressing like an elegant Parisian.

Art Deco graphics could be seen on paint brochures, dye catalogs, cookbooks, and first aid tins. The graphics helped to sell everything from typewriter ribbons and crepe paper to party favors and recipe books.

The Dennison Manufacturing Company, which started in 1844 by making jewelry boxes, had its headquarters in Framingham, Massachusetts. In 1898, it was the first American company to make paper boxes. Dennison's specialty was tags and they invented the reinforcements that kept the tags from tearing. They also manufactured gummed labels, tissue papers, and the first decorative crepe paper, which they began manufacturing in 1894. They started the gift-wrapping industry in this country, and were famous for their Christmas and holiday seals. Dennison's first catalogs were printed in the 1870s. All of the catalogs from then through the 1930s and1940s are very collectible today. The catalogs show how to make costumes and table decorations out of crepe paper.

The Dennison Company was bought by Avery International, a California-based company, in 1990 and most of its manufacturing moved out of Framingham.

The P. F. Volland Company was started in Chicago in 1908. It was known for its beautifully illustrated children's books. Volland used the best children's authors and illustrators of the time to produce books that would make children happy. This was their moral ideal and they carried it out faithfully, never publishing children's books that were frightening or showed cruelty. Unfortunately, they ceased publishing books in 1934. They also published a line of high-quality gift and recipe books, which came in boxes, that matched the vibrant, colorful book covers. Invitations, bridge tallies, and place cards all had wonderful Art Deco graphics and the Volland look of quality and style. They published lovely poetry books, baby books and a line of stationary. The Special Collection and Pres-

ervation Division of the Chicago Public Library has a very large and wonderful collection of Volland materials of all kinds.

This is one of the easiest types of great Art Deco graphics to find. Flea markets and antique shops and shows abound with old recipe and product booklets. As in every category, condition is most important. Is the cover on? Are pages torn or ripped out? Is it stained?

An abundance of beautifully illustrated recipe and appliance booklets produced by the food industry.

Recipe book. Radiation Ltd. 1935. England. $15-25.

Two recipe books. Left, Roberts & Mander Stove Company. 1936. Right, Frigidaire. 1933. $10-20 each.

Two recipe books. Left, Worcester Salt Company. 1937. Right, Ceresota Flour Company. $5-20 each.

Two Jello covers. Top, 1933. Bottom, 1930. $10-20 each.

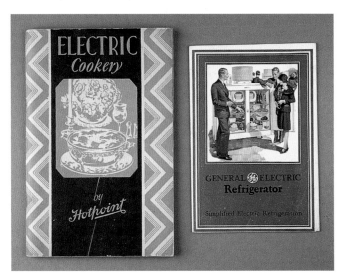

Two recipe books. Left, Hotpoint. 1929. Right, General Electric. 1929. $10-20 each.

Two Jello recipe books. Left, 1929. Right, 1933. $10-20 each.

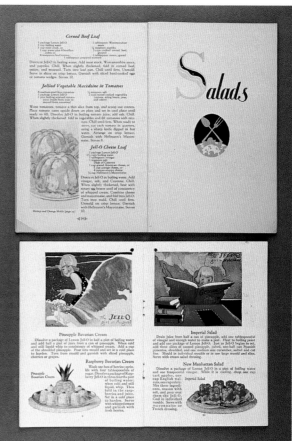

Illustrations from Jello books. Top, 1929. Bottom, 1924.

Five Jello recipe books. Top: left, 1924; right, 1917. Center: left, 1928; right, 1925, artist: L. Ball. Bottom: left, 1928, artist: Lucille Patterson Marsh; right, 1928. $10-20 each.

Two recipe books. Left, Royal Baking Powder Company. 1926. Right, General Mills. 1931. $15-25 each.

Illustration from Royal Baking Powder book. 1926.

Two cookbooks. Woman's World Magazine Company. Inc. 1927. Chicago. $15-25 each.

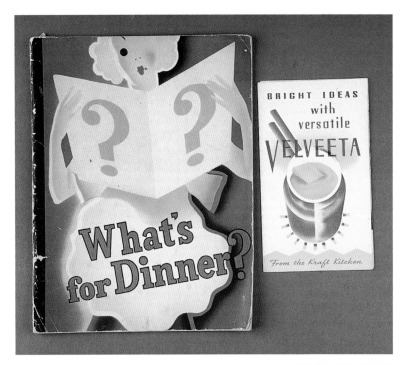

Two recipe books. Left, Merkel Inc. New York. Right, Kraft. $10-20 each.

Two recipe books. Left, William Griese Company. 1931. New Jersey. Right, Borden Sales Company. $10-20 each.

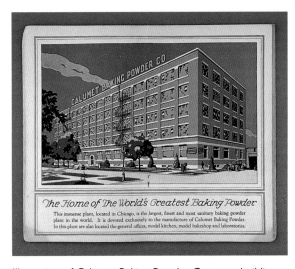

Illustration of Calumet Baking Powder Company building.

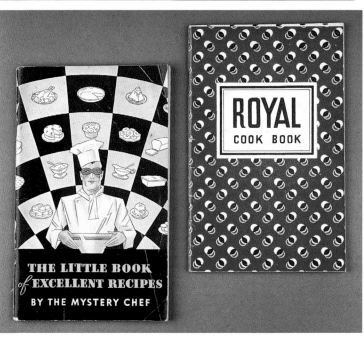

Two recipe books. Left, Davis Baking Powder Company. 1934. Right, Royal Baking Powder Company. 1939. $15-25 each.

Three recipe books. Top, Kraft 1933. Left, Avon. 1938. Right, Hotpoint. 1928. $10-20 each.

Two health books. Left, B. St. John Doherty, artist: J.G. England. Right, The Illinois Herb Company. 1933. $10-25 each.

Two recipe books. Left, The Radiation Co., Ltd. Right, Hugon and Company. Ltd. 1933. Both from England. $10-20 each.

These cookbook covers and boxes are works of art!

Cookbook and matching box. The Calendar of Luncheons Teas
and Suppers. P.F. Volland Company. Joliet, Illinois. $45-70.

Two cookbooks. Left, The Calendar of Sandwiches &
Beverages. Right, The Calendar of Cakes Fillings and
Frostings. P.F. Volland Company. Chicago. $30-45 each.

Cookbook and matching box. New Calendar of
Salads. P.F. Volland Company. Chicago. $45-70.

Cookbook and matching box. Satisfying Salads, artist Carrie Dudley. A.G. Volland and the Buzza Company. Craftacres Minneapolis. $50-70.

Cookbook and matching box. Luscious Luncheons and Tasty Teas, artist: Carrie Dudley. A.G. Volland and the Buzza Company. Craftacres Minneapolis. $50-70.

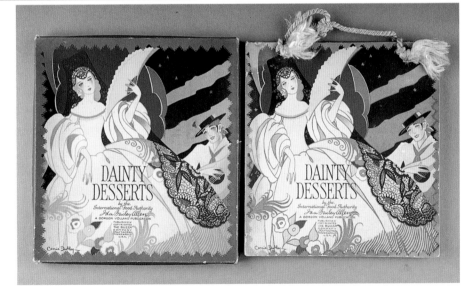

Cookbook and matching box. Dainty Desserts, artist: Carrie Dudley. A. G. Volland and the Buzza Company. Craftacres Minneapolis. $50-70.

Cake decorator set and birthday candles. Left and top right, Candle-Lite, Inc. Bottom right, Candle Craft. Center, no maker marked. $10-20 each.

Another area where Art Deco graphics were use in the
home decoration and paint industry.

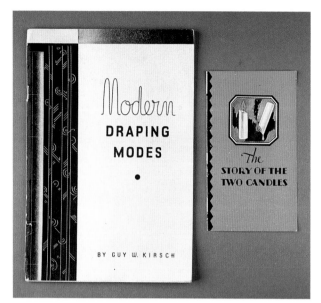

Two booklets. Left, Kirsch Company. 1934. Right, Iron
Fireman Manufacturing Company. 1928. $10-20 each.

Catalog. Modern Steel Equipment Company. $15-35.

Illustration from Dutch Boy Paint catalog. 1929. $15-35.

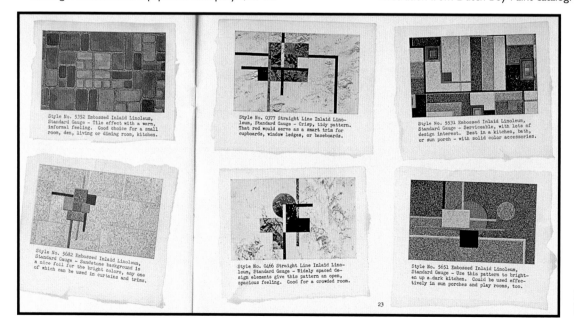

Illustration from Armstrong
Linoleum catalog. 1944. $15-35.

Illustration from Dutch Boy Paint catalog. 1929.

Three paint brochures. Devoe & Raynolds, Inc. 1938. $15-30 each.

Three paint brochures. Left, Lus-Tro-Lac. Center, Sherwin Williams. 1937. Right, Wetherill & Company. $15-30 each.

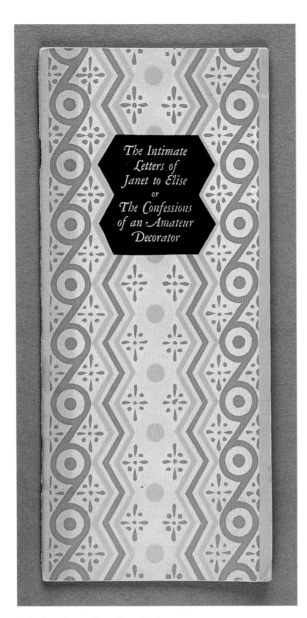

Paint brochure. The Egyptian Lacquer
Company. New York. $15-35.

Paint brochure. Sherwin Williams. 1936. $15-35.

Paint brochure. Sherwin Williams. 1935. $15-35.

Illustration from The Egyptian
Lacquer Company brochure.

Paint and decorating catalog cover. Artist:
Rockwell Kent. Sherwin Williams. 1936. $35-50.

DECORATIVE CHARACTER
IN BATHROOMS

Ceiling and Bath Recess—Mello-Gloss Aqua Green.
Walls—Mello-Gloss Light Canary.

Illustration from paint catalog.
Lowe Brothers. 1935. $15-30.

Back cover of Sherwin Williams catalog.

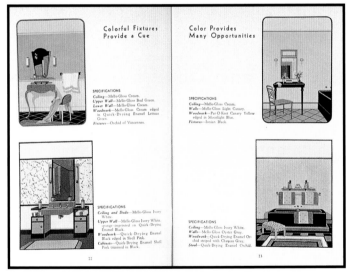

Illustration from Lowe Brothers catalog.

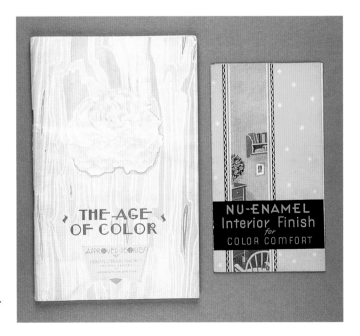

Booklet cover. Left, flower catalog. Indian Spring Farms.
1928. Right, paint brochure. Nu-Enamel Corp. $15-35.

The area of home entertainment and parties produced some wonderful ephemera. Many of these were published by The Dennison Company.

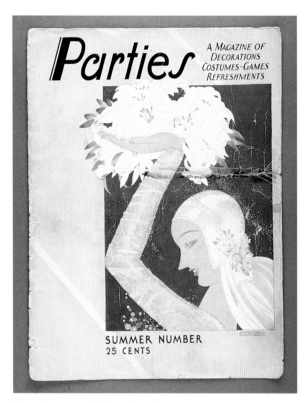

Magazine cover. Parties. Dennison Manufacturing Company. 1930. $15-30.

Three cocktail booklets. Left, The Mixer House. Portland , Oregon. Right two not marked. $5-20 each.

Three booklet covers. Left, 1929. Center, 1920. Right, 1925. All from Dennison's. $5-45 each.

Two booklet covers. Left, 1930, Dennison's.
Right, 1931, Dennison's England. $15-30 each.

Magazine cover. *Party Magazine*. Artist:
Holm Gren. Dennison's. 1927. $25-50.

Here are some more great examples of advertising and packaging using Art Deco graphics.

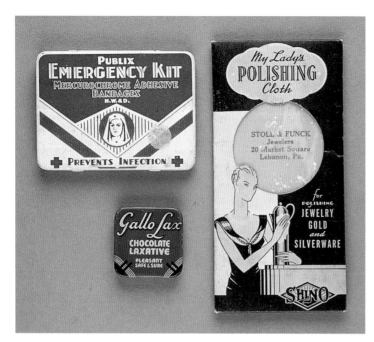

Top left, first aid tin, Northeastern Laboratory, Boston. Bottom left, laxative tin, P.H. Galloway Ltd., London. Right, Shino polishing cloth. $5-20 each

Sewing book. Simplicity Pattern Company. 1932. $15-35.

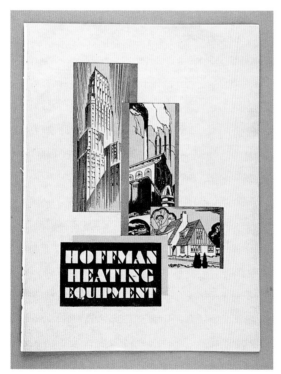

Catalog. Hoffman Heating Company. 1932. $15-35.

Four typewriter ribbon tins. Top: left, Bronx Typewriter Exchange; right, Kee Lox Manufacturing Company. Bottom: left, Old Town Ribbon and Carbon Company; right, True Mark Brand. $10-50 each.

Six typewriter ribbon tins. Top: left, Underwood; center, American Writing Machine Company; right, Columbia. Bottom: left and center, Underwood; right, Empress. $5-25 each.

Two shoe products. Left and center, Glace by Everett & Barron Company. Right, Shinola shoe shine kit. $5-20 each.

Left, Kroma crayons, The American Crayon Company. Top right, clay, Creston Crayon Company. Bottom, licorice box, Banner Candy Company. $5-20 each.

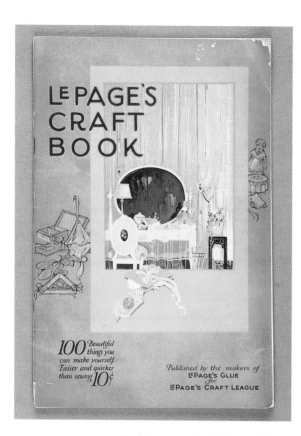

Left:
Booklet cover. LePage's Glue. Russia Cement Company. 1924. $15-30.

Illustration from Le Page's booklet.

Booklet covers. Left, Diamond Dyes. 1926. Right, Dye-O-La Dye Company. 1926. $15-35 each.

With Diamond Dyes

[Page Forty-nine]

Illustration from Diamond Dye catalog.

Above and below:
Illustration from Dye-O-La Dye Company catalog.

COLOR CRAFT

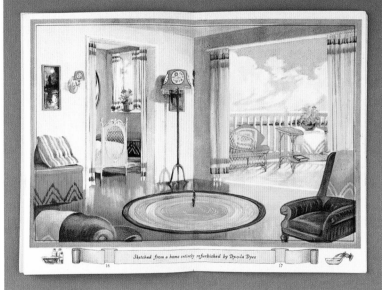

Booklet cover. Diamond Dye catalog.

Chapter 4
Art

There is, of course, a whole world of incredible Art Deco painting, watercolors, posters and more to be found in museums, art galleries, and at large auction houses. For our purposes, however, there are also many wonderful examples of the graphic art of the era that are affordable and easily obtainable. Magazines from the 1920s and 1930s abound with great designs especially on the covers, which were created by many of the famous artists of the period. Some dealers sell just the covers already framed. Book jackets from old novels, whether they were created by famous illustrators like Rockwell Kent or unknowns, can be found in most second hand bookstores. There were many unknown artists of the time who designed colorful and appealing book jackets.

Among the easily found and inexpensive art items are book covers, sheet music, catalog covers, old yearbooks, menus, trade magazines, labels and box wrappers, and even old schoolbooks. Prices vary widely due to many variables. Is it an original signed piece? Is the book a first edition? Did the artist do special editions? I have not included magazine covers or art removed from a book or magazine. All the prices are for complete works.

This is a category where condition really counts in the value. Beware of water stains and mildew, torn and missing pages, and use your nose! The odor of must and mildew stands out and I have not been successful in getting rid of it.

Rockwell Kent was born in New York in 1882. Although he was best known for his wood cut book illustrations, he was also a painter, did advertisements for large companies, designed stamps and Christmas cards, and did industrial design for the Chase Metal Company.

Lynd Ward was born in Chicago in 1905. He studied in Germany and among his well known early works were books that were totally illustrated without words. These examples show a dark side to the artist but he went on to become a very successful illustrator of children's books, some of which he also wrote.

John Austen was born in England in 1886. His many illustrated books show a contrast in technique from dark and foreboding to subtle lines of color.

Vibrant and interesting graphics in book and magazine illustration were used by unknown and famous artists alike. These are some of the finest examples of the era.

Magazine cover. *Art-Goute-Beauté*. Christmas 1922.

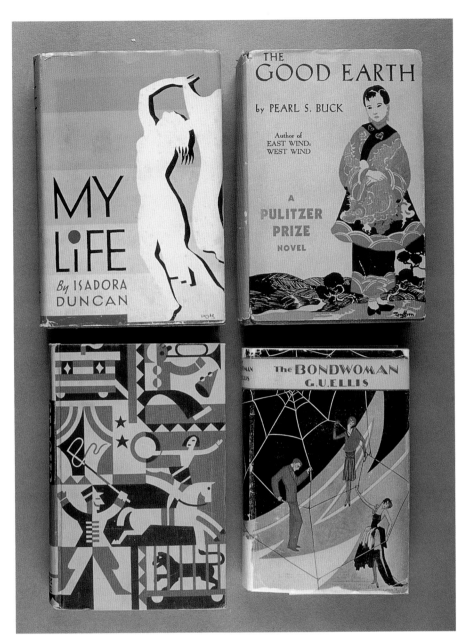

Four book covers. Top left, *My Life*, artist: Sugar. 1927. Top right, *The Good Earth*, artist: Gustav Tenggren. 1934. Bottom left, *Circus Shoes*, artist: Richard Floethe. 1939. Bottom right, *The Bondwoman*, artist: Letherts. 1927. $10-25 each.

Children Across the Sea

...ly and Bob were going on a voyage around the world with their father and mother on the yacht *Sea Gull*. They ...y happy for now they would see how children lived in other lands.

...en everybody was on board and everything was ready, they watched the sailors in their places heave up the anchor ...st the white sails. Then the wind filled the sails and the ship headed for the open sea. Judy and Bob were off on ...st long voyage.

...et's climb the ropes and wave to the people on shore," ...b, and up he scrambled.

...ly held on tight with both hands and shouted, "Good-bye! ...ye!" But Bob was used to climbing and he let go with one ...d waved his cap in farewell.

...e ship drew farther and farther from the shore and soon ...d Bob could not see the people. But they stayed up in the ...for a long time watching the sea gulls fly around.

...ok at that gull! See how it slides right along the water!" ...ed Bob, pointing out a large white one.

...think that is why our boat is called the *Sea Gull*," his ...id. "It slides over the ocean just like the birds, and it is ...oo."

...nly we don't fly around in the air like they do," sighed ...Wish we did!"

...do too," said Judy. "But oh my, I am hungry! Let's go ...o the kitchen and get something to eat."

...n a ship, a kitchen is called a galley," corrected her brother ...climbed down the ropes.

Book illustration from *Children Across the Sea*.
Artist: Janet Laura Scott. 1931. $15-25.

On the Other Side of the World

"What time is it, Captain?" Bob asked as they climbed into the ship's boat that was to take them ashore.

"Nine o'clock in the morning in China," he answered, putting special emphasis on "in the morning."

"Oh, I know what you are thinking," volunteered Judy. "It's not in the morning at home. It is night. All the boys and girls there are going to bed. We are on the other side of the world!"

As they rowed across the harbor, they looked at the strange boats. There were large ones and small ones. Some were house boats, and people lived on them. The Captain said the large ships were called junks.

The Captain had a special treat for Bob and Judy. He took them to a Chinese school. They found the Chinese boys and girls didn't have desks or books like theirs. And the writing was so queer! Bob couldn't tell which was right side up.

Book illustration from *Children Across the Sea*.

Book illustration from *Alice Au Pas des Merveilles*. Artist: A. Pécoud. 1935. France.

Book illustrations from *Manon Lescaut*. Artist: John Austen. London. 1928. $150-350.

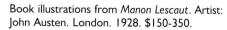

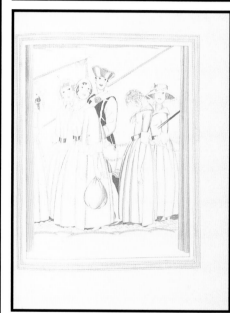

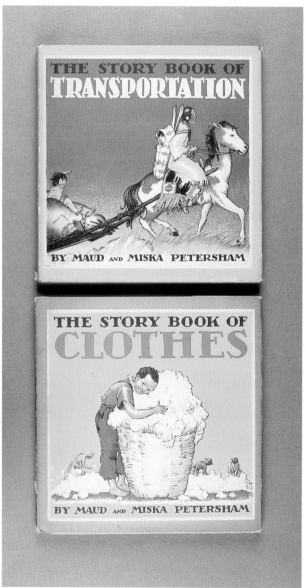

Book covers. Top, *The Story Book of Transportation*. Bottom, *The Story Book of Clothes*. Both by Maud and Misha Petersham. 1933. $10-125 each.

Book illustrations from *N by E* by
Rockwell Kent. 1930. $25-350.

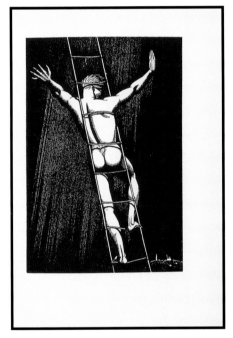

Book illustration from *The Mimes
of the Courtesans*, artist: Charles
Cullen. 1931. $25-100.

Book illustration from *The
Mimes of the Courtesans*.

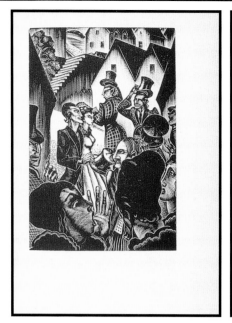

Book illustrations from *Mad Man's Drum*.

Cover of *The Savoy Cocktail Book*. Artist:
Gilbert Rumbold. 1930. $200-400.

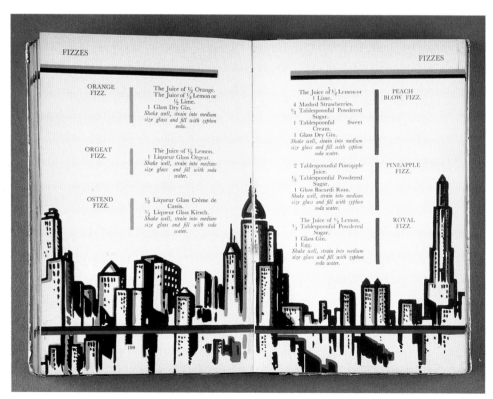

Book illustration from
The Savoy Cocktail Book.

Cover of *Mad Man's Drum*.
Artist: Lynd Ward. 1930.
$100-600.

Left and above:
Book illustration from *God's Man*,
by Lynd Ward. 1929. $100-1800.

Book cover and box from *Mother*.
Artist: Maurine Hathaway. 1926. The
Buzza Company. $25-50.

Book illustration from *Mother*.

Decorative leather book cover.

Book cover. *Zest*, cover by
Rockwell Kent. 1934. $15-45.

Scrapbook. *School Days*. Gibson Art Company. $15-50.

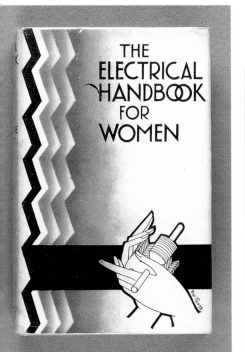

Cover of *The Electrical Handbook for Women*.
Artist: Bip Pares. 1939. London. $15-30.

Yearbook cover. *Comus* Allentown, Pennsylvania. 1933.

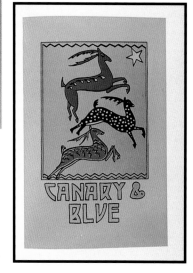

Illustration from the *Comus*.

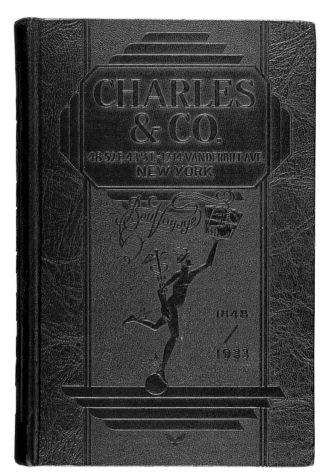

Book cover. Catalog for Charles &
Company. New York. 1933. $15-75.

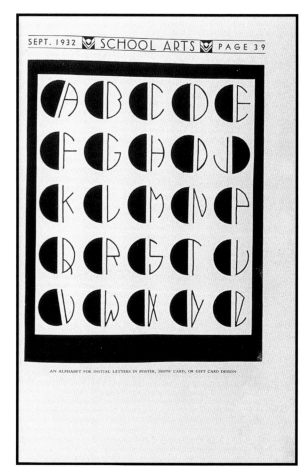

An Art Deco alphabet. *School Arts* magazine.

Two alphabets. *School Arts*
magazine. 1932. $5-10.

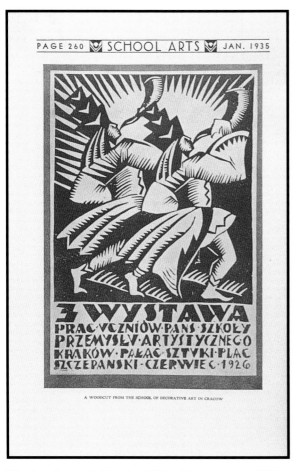

A WOODCUT FROM THE SCHOOL OF DECORATIVE ART IN CRACOW

Woodcut from a Polish school. *School Arts* magazine. 1935.

Yearbook art done by students. *School Arts* magazine.

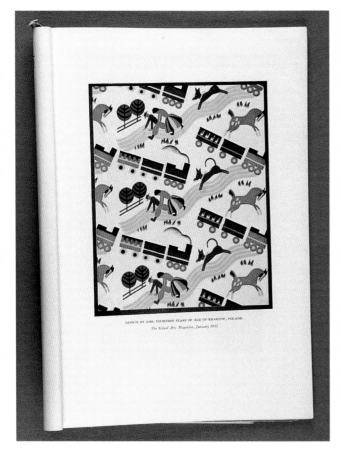

Art from a 14 year old Polish girl. *School Arts* magazine.

Three coloring books. Artist: Roberto Ugrilli. 1943. Italy. $5-12 each.

Four book covers. Top left, *The Outdoor Girls in the Air*. 1932. Top right, *Pinocchio*. Bottom left, *Janet Hardy in Hollywood*. Artist: Two Taylors. 1935. Bottom right, *Jane, Stewardess of the Air Lines*. Artist: Two Taylors. 1934. $10-25 each.

Here are some very Deco sheet music covers and motto.

Sheet music cover. *My Darling*, artist: Jorg Harris. 1932. $5-10.

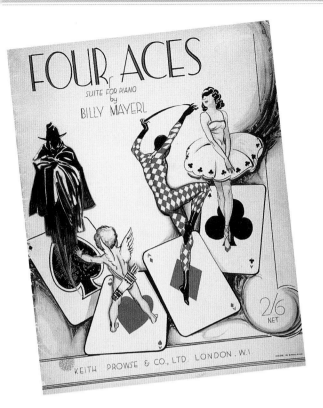

Sheet music cover. *Four Aces*. England. $10-25.

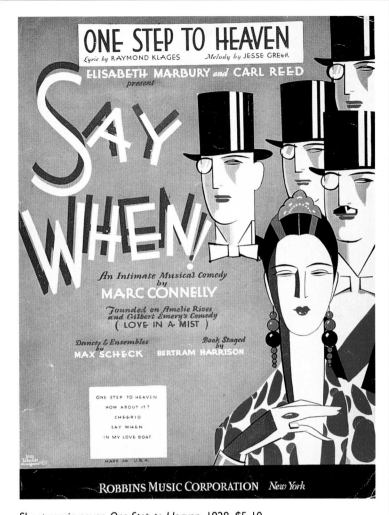

Sheet music cover. *One Step to Heaven*. 1928. $5-10.

Sheet music cover. *Until the Real Thing
Comes Along*, artist: Jorg Harris. 1936. $5-10.

Sheet music cover. *All Aboard for
Heaven*, artist: Leff. 1925. $15-25.

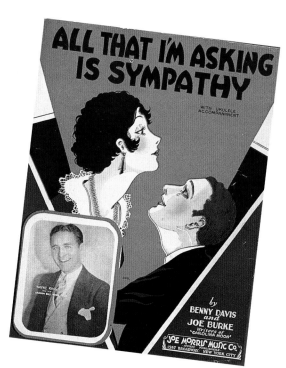

Sheet music cover. *All That I'm Asking is Sympathy*, artist: Earl. 1929. $5-10.

Sheet music cover. *The Gypsy*. 1945. $5-10.

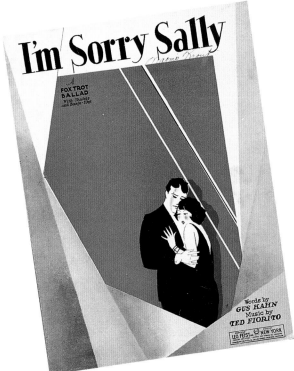

Sheet music cover. *I'm Sorry Sally*. 1928. $5-10.

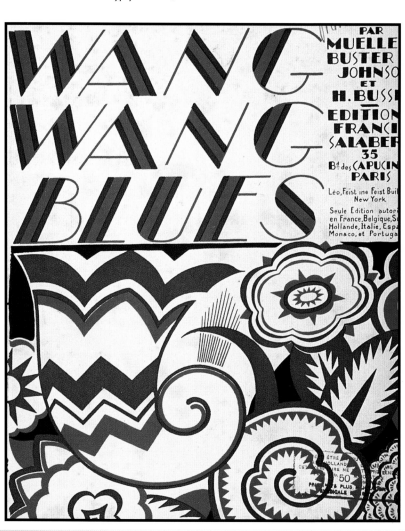

Sheet music cover. *Wang Wang Blues*. France. $5-10.

Framed motto. *It's Queer*, artist: Maurine Hathaway. 1925. The Buzza Company. $20-40.

The house of Jeanne Lanvin in Paris commissioned Jean Duché, among others, to do a series of box labels for perfumes, gift boxes, beauty products and candy boxes in 1925.

The use of beautiful graphics for candy box labels and wrappers was very popular in Europe. Menu art was another area of great graphics.

Art for box labels. France. $10-20 each.

Art for box label. France. $15-50.

Art for label. France. $10-35.

107

Box label for baby gift. Artist: L. Bonnotte. 1925. Belgium. $25-50.

Presentation box label for Maison Jeanne Lanvin. Artist: Jean Duché. France. $25-50.

Box label for baby gift. Artist: L. Bonnotte. 1925. Belgium. $25-50.

Presentation box label for Maison Jeanne Lanvin. $25-50.

Hand painted candy box. England. $35-100.

Artists in the United States and Europe designed a variety
of terrific magazine covers and hand-colored plates.

Magazine cover. *Child Life*. Artist: Hazel Frazee. 1926. $8-18.

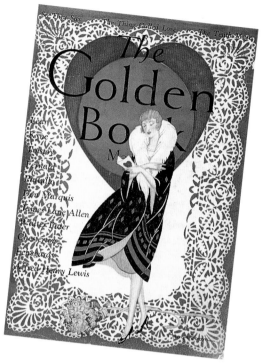

Magazine cover. *The Golden Book*.
Artist: Hogeboom. 1927. $10-20.

Magazine cover. *More Business*.
Artist: Coutré Erman. 1936. $10-20.

Magazine cover. *The Dance*. Artist: Gigi Shaule Johnson. 1931. $10-20.

Magazine cover. *Garden and Home Builder*. Artist: Eleanor Custis. 1927. $15-25.

Magazine cover. *Garden and Home Builder*. Artist: Marion T. Justice. 1926. $15-25.

Large hand-colored picture for a box label. Artist: Ginot. France. $20-100.

Hand-colored plate. Artist:
Tito. Translation: *Words spoken
fly away, those written down
remain.* France. $100-300.

Hand-colored plate. Artist: S. Soura
Créco. France. $100-300.

New Year's Invitation.
Hand-colored original
plate. 1938. England.

Invitation. Hand-colored. $15-45.

Four hand painted postcards. Artist: Susie. France. $15-25.

Smokers by Janine Aghion.
Original plate. 1920. France.

Two calendar backs. France. $15-35 each.

Two calendar backs. France. $15-35 each.

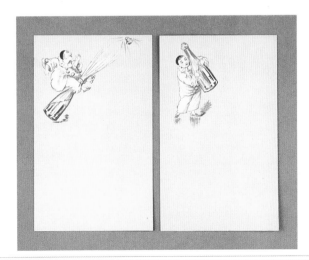

Menu cards for champagne.
France. $10-45 each.

Menu cards. France. $15-45 each.

Menu art. France. $15-25.

Three menu cards. France. $15-45 each.

Left, Menu, artist: Napoli. France. Right, postcard. 1934. France. $10-30 each.

Menu art. France. $15-25.

Hand painted box label. Artist:
Ginot. France. $35-75.

This is an original commemorative diploma from the Arts Decoratifs Industriels Modernes Paris 1925. It was for the Czeckoslovakian section of Class 28 given to R. Kepl.

Original commemorative diploma given to R. Kepl of the Czechoslovakian section at the *Exposition International des Arts Decoratifs et Industriels Modernes* Paris 1925. Artist: Rigal. France.

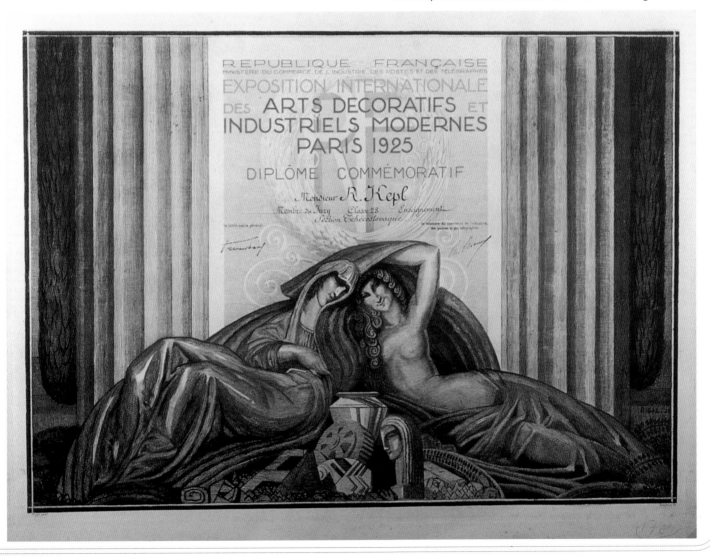

Chapter 5
Fashion

The origins of Deco design in the fashion industry are found in France in the early part of the century. From 1900 until 1925 more than 20 French houses of *haute couture* opened their doors. The look they produced for women was sensual, elegant, sleek and sexy. The influence of Léon Bakst's extravagant and exciting sets and costumes for the Ballets Russes in 1908, was the beginning of an era for French fashion and its illustrators. Paul Poiret, who was the leading fashion designer of the time, hired Paul Iribe and, then, Georges Lepape to illustrate his fashions in individual albums. These became very popular and led to a flourishing of French fashion design and illustration by George Barbier, André Marty, Charles Martin, Erté, Éduard Halouze, and many others.

The major Paris department stores like *Au Printemps* and *Galeries Lafayette* employed designers to illustrate their catalogs and do their window displays. The influences on French Art Deco fashion came from as far away as Turkey, Asia, Africa, and the Jazz Age in America.

French fashion magazines such as *Gazette du Bon Ton, Journal des Dames et des Modes, Modes et Manierères d' Aujourd'hui, Art-Goût-Beauté,* and *femina* used all the most talented fashion illustrators to draw the best and most fabulous fashions of the day. These magazines used the pochoir process to reproduce the illustrations. This time-consuming process was all done by hand. Stencils were made of copper or zinc and cut out. As many as thirty plates at a time were used to build up the color, producing a very exact replication of the original art. The backgrounds of these fashion illustrations were as colorful and intricate as the designs themselves.

Designers like Lepape and Iribe also designed for *Vogue* and *Harper's Bazaar.* Lepape did poster, fashion, and set design. George Barbier was a book and magazine illustrator who went into fashion and costume design. He also designed wallpaper, fabrics and theater programs.

Janine Aghion was a fashion designer and illustrator and a painter.

Eduardo Garcia Benito was born in Spain but came to France to do fashion and book illustration.

Ettore Tito also came to Paris to do fashion illustration. He was born in Italy.

The items included in this chapter can be found at flea markets, paper shows, auctions, and antique shops. It is, of course, easier and sometimes less expensive to find French magazines in France, but they are available in the United States. Other items in the fashion category that are easily found are buttons on store cards, fans, store brochures, and advertising. A double find is a pochoir illustration of a famous designer such as Jeanne Lanvin, done by a famous illustrator like George Barbier.

Prices in this category vary according to condition as with all paper. If it is a magazine, is it complete? Is the cover by a known artist? Is it artist signed? If it is a fan, is it artist signed? Is the fan common or rare? The original plates vary in price according to artist and if it is signed. Fashion catalogs are easy to find. There are some great examples of Art Deco graphics in the catalogs from the United States as well as France. Many dealers frame the magazine covers or tear out and frame the pochoirs from the French magazines. These prices vary.

Nowhere else will you find more beautiful examples of Art Deco graphics than in the fashion industry. Fashion magazines and department stores in the United States and Europe put out many publications, advertisements, and advertising fans. Even the button manufacturers used Art Deco graphics on their store cards. Most of the fashion industry was geared toward women.

Hand painted plate for Gotham silk hosiery.
Artist: Hoffe. France. $100-300.

Dress design by Henriette Boudreaux. *femina*. 1932. France.

Cover of catalog for *La
Place Clichy*. Paris. $45-80.

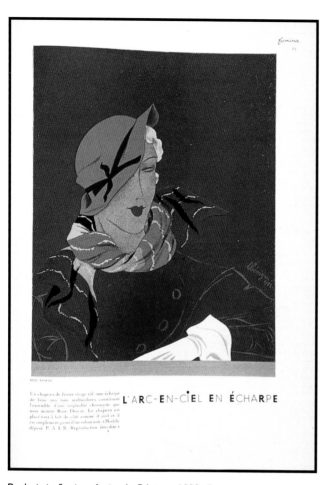

Pochoir in *femina*. Artist: L. Bénigni. 1932. France.

Cover of catalog for *Au Printemps*. Artist: Benito. 1921. Paris. $45-80.

Catalog for *Chaussures Raoul* shoes. 1926. France.

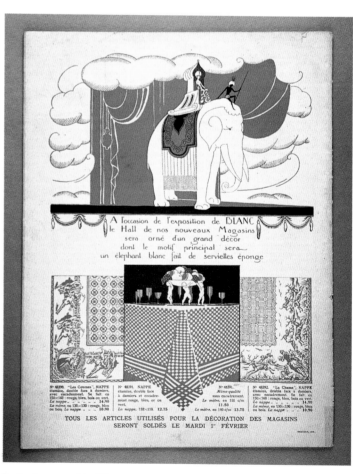

Back of cover of *Au Printemps*.

Fashion advertising fan. *Au Printemps*.
Artist: V. Espi. Paris. $75-300.

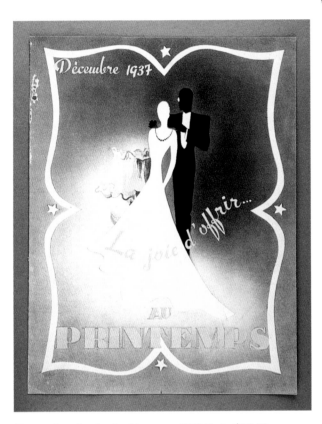

Cover of catalog for *Au Printemps*. 1937. Paris. $25-50.

Cover of catalog for *Aux Trois Quartiers*.

Centerfold pochoir from *Art-Goût-Beauté* featuring the following designers: Jean Patou, Douellet, Martial et Armand, and Jeanne Lanvin. 1924. Paris.

119

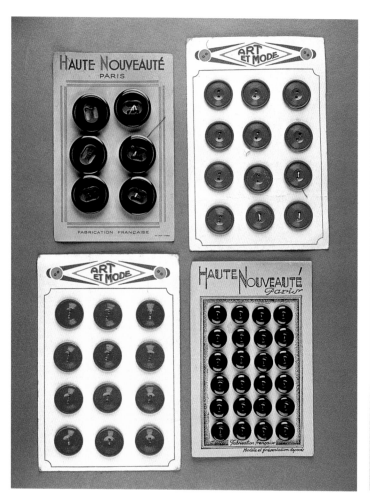

Buttons on store cards. France. $5-20 each.

Cover of catalog for *Galeries Lafayette*.
Artist: Benito. 1939. Paris. $45-80.

Fashion advertising fan. *Galeries Lafayette*.
Artist: Jack Roberto. Paris. $75-300.

Fashion advertising fan from *Galeries Lafayette*.
Front, artist: Gabriel Ferro. Paris. $75-300.

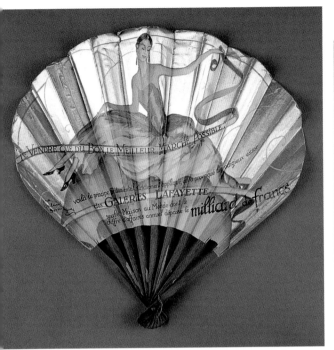

Back of fan. Artist: Jean Gabriel Dominique.

Cover of catalog for *La Samaritaine*. Paris. $45-75.

Pochoir from *Art-Goût-Beauté* featuring fashions by
Philippe et Gaston and Paul Poiret. 1924. Paris.

Cover of catalog for *La Samaritaine*. Paris. $45-75.

Cover of catalog for *La Samaritaine*. Paris. $45-75.

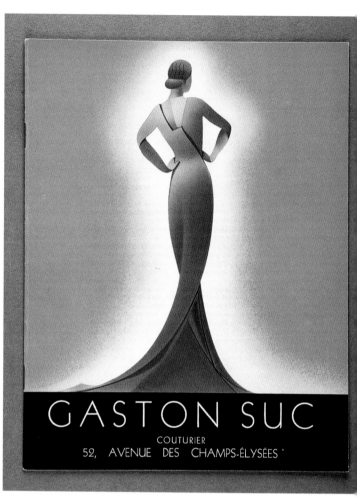

Catalog for *Gaston Suc* dressmaker. Paris. $25-50.

Cover of accessories catalog for *La Samaritaine*. 1929. Paris. $35-75.

Cover of accessories catalog for *Au Louvre*. Artist: A. E. Marty. Paris. $40-80.

Fashion advertising fan. *Au Bon Marché*. Paris. $75-300.

Catalog cover. *Au Bon Marché*. 1931. Paris.

Back of fan. Artist: Loubok.

Illustration from *Art-Goût-Beauté*. 1925. Paris.

Here are some examples of Art Deco graphics used in children's fashions.

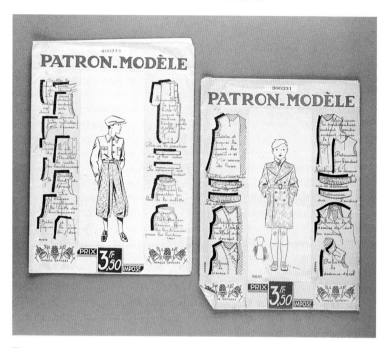

Two clothing patterns for boys. France. $5-15 each.

Cover of children's Christmas catalog from *Chez Jones*. 1937. Paris. $10-35.

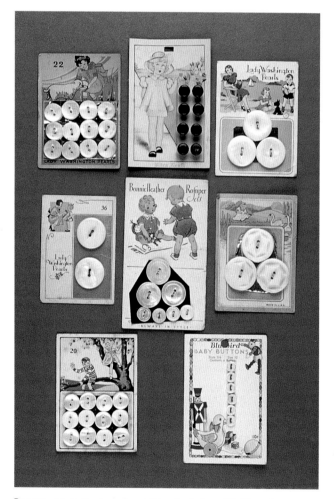

Buttons on store cards for children's clothes. $5-12 each.

Cover of Jouets Etrennés Christmas gift catalog from *Au Louvre*. 1936. Paris. $35-75.

Cover of First Communion clothing catalog
from *Belle Jardiniere*. 1939. Paris. $15-40.

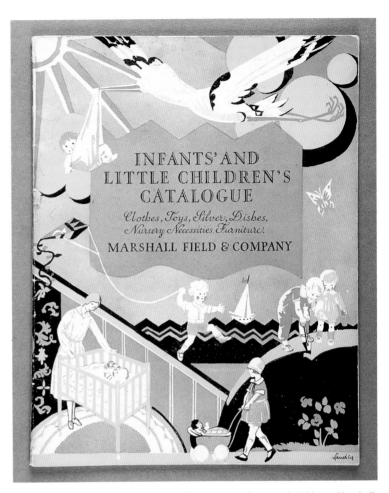

Catalog for infants and children. *Marshall,
Field and Company*. Chicago. $45-75.

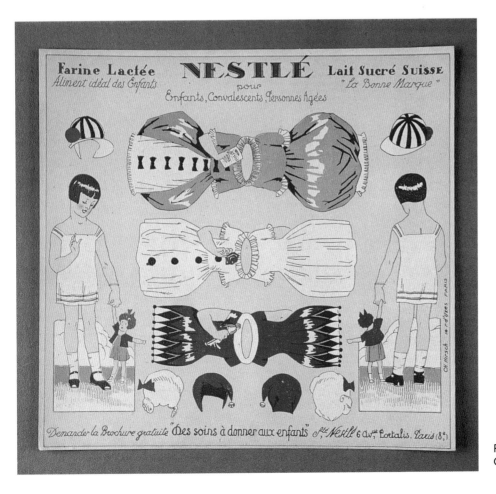

Paper dolls. The Nestlé
Company. Paris. $35-50.

Illustration from *Au Printemps* catalog.

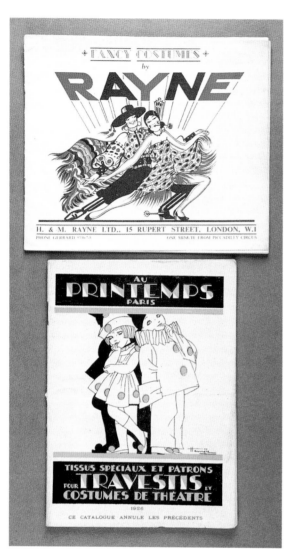

Two costume catalogs. Top, *Rayne*. 1935.
London. Bottom, *Au Printemps*, artist:
Hennjie. 1926. Paris. $25-50 each.

Illustration from *Au Printemps* catalog.

Some more beautiful advertising for women's fashion.

Centerfold pochoir from *Art-Goût-Beauté* featuring fashions by Doeuillet, Doucet, Jeanne Halleé, and Madelaine et Madelaine. 1923. Paris.

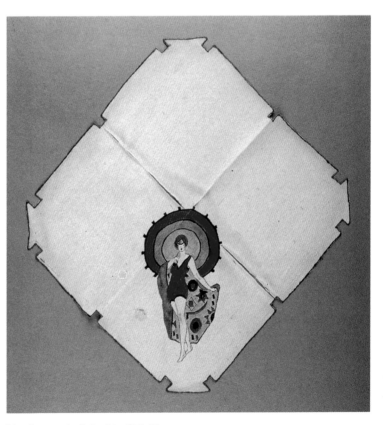

Back cover of catalog for *Aux Trois Quartiers*.
Artist: Mariane Andren. 1936. Paris. $40-75.

Hand painted silk hankie. $15-45.

Hat box. France. $50-75.

Four boxes for the Paris Garter Company. U.S. $25-75 each.

Three handkerchief boxes each.

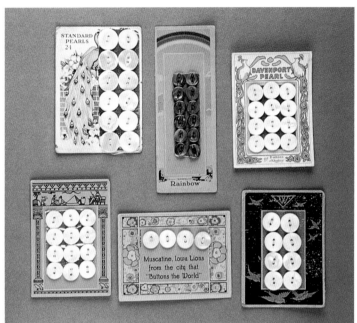

More buttons on store cards. $5-12 each.

Buttons on store cards. The cards have illustrations with Art Deco graphics. $8-18 each.

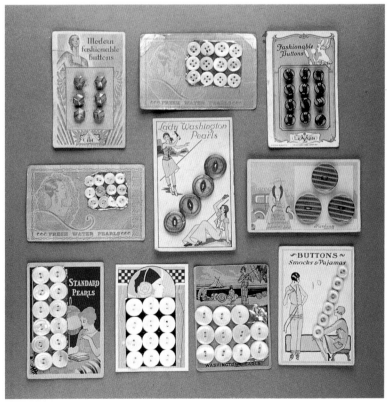

Buttons on store cards featuring women. $5-12 ea

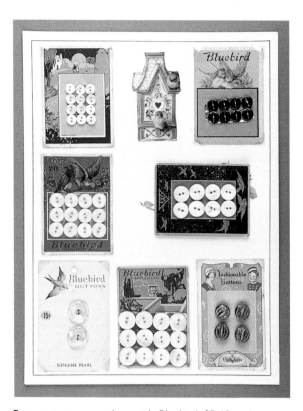

Buttons on store cards, mostly Bluebird. $5-12 each.

Two hat boxes. The top box depicts different cities in the United States. The bottom example is for La Rose Hats, Owen, Moore & Company. Portland, Maine. $50-75 each.

Handkerchief from the movie *Top Hat*. 1935. $45-75.

Fashion advertising fan.
Bonwit Teller. $50-150.

Left:
Cover of catalog for *B. Altman and Company*. 1927. New York.

Illustration from *B. Altman* catalog.

Cover of catalog for *Lord & Taylor*.
Christmas 1937. New York. $25-75.

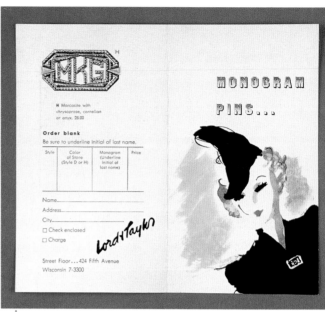

Order form for marcasite monogram pins from *Lord & Taylor* catalog.

Endpaper from *Art-Goût-Beauté*. 1924. Paris.

These have included some men.

Cover of catalog for *Belle Jardiniére*. Artist, René Vincent. 1935. Paris. $40-80.

Back cover of *Belle Jardiniére*.

Cover of catalog for *Belle Jardinière*. Artist: Guy Sabran. 1936. Paris. $40-75.

Cover of catalog for *Réaumur*. 1936. Paris. $35-75.

Back cover of *Belle Jardinière*.

Back cover of *Réaumur*.

Mostly for men.

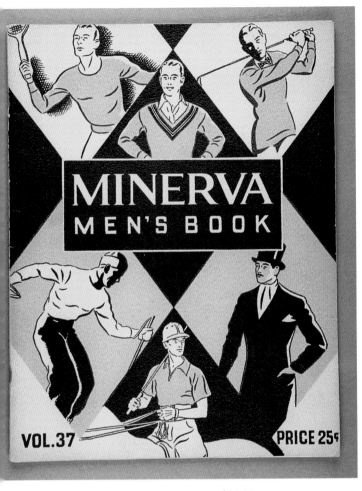

Catalog cover. *Minerva Yarn Company.* 1934. $20-35.

Brochure for Maurel Fréres & Cie raincoats. 1936. Paris. $35-75.

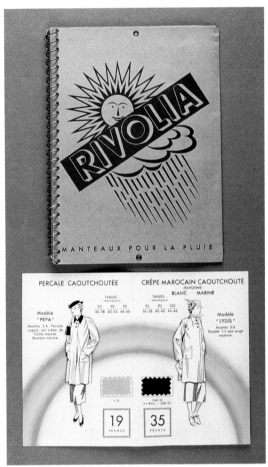

Left, catalog for Conchon-Quinette clothing. 1929. Right, catalog for Henri Esders. 1928. Both France. $25-50 each.

Three men's fashion catalogs. France. $25-50 each.

Buttons on store cards for men's clothes. $5-20 each.

Hand painted original plate. Artist: Éduard Halouze. Paris. $100-300.

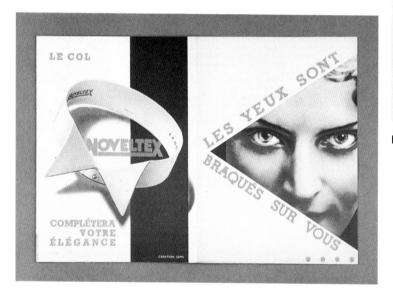

Cover of brochure for Novetex men's shirt collars. Artist: Sepio. France. $5-20.

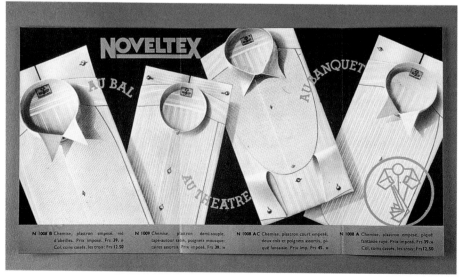

Inside of brochure for Novetex.

Chapter 6
Cosmetics

The idea of makeup, and the packaging and selling of it, was very popular in France in the 1920s and 1930s. The large department stores like Galeries Lafayette and Au Printemps had their own designers who created the incredible Art Deco designs for their displays and their products. The bright and bold designs of the packaging of perfume and other beauty products led women to believe that what was inside the package, whether creams, lipsticks, perfumes, or powder, would make them look as beautiful as the package implied. Even in that time period, millions of dollars were spent on the packaging and promoting the idea of looking beautiful. It wasn't long before the cosmetic industry was big business in the United States as well.

Brand names evolved from the perfume companies. They developed their own lines of cosmetics and competed in this constantly changing industry by trying to design the most daring and visible boxes. The graphics depicted sleek, stylized women, often nude or scantily dressed. The bright colors, the streamlined designs, and the idea of being beautiful inspired the manufacturers to keep up with the style trends and to stay ahead of the increasingly competitive market.

The cosmetics were accompanied by wonderfully designed booklets describing the benefits of the products. It made no difference if you were a woman living in Paris, New York, or the American Midwest ; the assumption behind the cosmetics industry the same: what you looked like on the outside was the most important thing. It was this idea that the graphic designs of the times used to sell the products.

Hollywood also had a major influence on the cosmetic industry. Cosmetic companies encouraged the consumer to believe that, if you bought their products, you could be as slim, sexy and absolutely glamorous as that beautiful starlet on the screen. Like Greta Garbo or Carole Lombard, you could seduce your lover, and your life would have a happy ending, just like in the movies. The Art Deco sets of the movies of the time, such as "Top Hat" with Ginger Rogers and Fred Astaire, epitomized the luxury and sleek elegance of the Art Deco era.

Alexander Napolean Bourjois started his perfume house in Paris in the 1860s. Although he developed many fragrances, it was "Evening in Paris" and its striking cobalt blue bottle designed by Jean Helleu in 1928 that made the company famous.

Henri Bendel, who was born in Louisiana, opened his store on 57th Street in New York City in 1912. It was there that he started selling French couture clothing and perfume to New York's society women. He also developed his own line of perfume and cosmetics.

Richard Hudnut was the son of a New York druggist, whose store had opened in 1880. He was a man of class and style and was forward thinking. After a trip to Paris he changed his father's drug store into an upscale salon to sell his perfume and cosmetic products. The first perfume he developed, "Violet Sec," was very popular as was "Three Flowers," which debuted in 1915. Business was so successful that he sold the shop in 1916. Eleven years later, in 1927, he opened his beautiful and elegant Paris shop. From compacts to perfume gift sets, the Art Deco packaging and design of his products were a major selling point.

Other very successful companies, like Lander, Helena Rubenstein, Yardley, Max Factor and Tokalon, also had great Deco designed packaging.

Lander was founded as a budget-priced company in America in 1920 by Charles Oestreich and his partners. His use of beautiful graphics made his products look more expensive than they really were.

Helena Rubenstein was one of eight children born in Poland. She moved to Australia when she was 20 and opened her first beauty salon in Melbourne in 1902. It was a great success and she left Australia and opened her Paris salon in 1912. That was followed with a New York salon in 1915. Her "Valaze" line was presented at the 1925 Paris Exhibition.

In 1770 Thomas Yardley established his company in London. It lasted well into the 20th century making it one of the longest lasting companies in this industry.

Tokalon was originally an English company that moved to Paris. It is known for its phenomenal graphics.

The pricing in this category depends on a number of things. Is the item in the original box? What is the condition of the item? What is the condition of the box? If it is a powder box, has it been opened or is it still sealed? If it is a perfume bottle, has it been opened?

Packaging and advertising, were the keys to selling products
in the cosmetic industry. Here are some great examples.

Original art charcoal and pastel for a powder box. $50-75.

Store display for Eberhard Faber eyebrow pencils. Germany. $50-125.

Top three, "Wink" mascara sets. Ross Company.
New York City. Bottom, "I-Sheen" mascara tin set
by Kenra, Indianapolis, Indiana. $15-30 each.

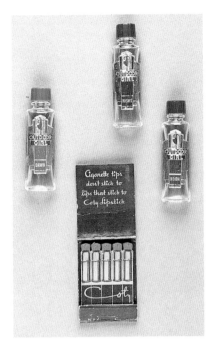

Three cologne bottles. Outdoor Girl. Matches advertising Coty lipstick. $15-25 each.

Mondaine leather vanity book, 1928. $75-125.

Six incense containers. A.A. Vantine & Company. New York. $15-25 each.

Calendar for Perfumeria Bellger. Artist: G. Camps. Barcelona. 1935. $35-50.

Another calendar for Perfumeria Bellger. Artist: G. Camps. 1935.

Max Factor brochures, numbers one to four, and
a catalog for Max Factor's theatrical make-up.

Max Factor brochures, numbers five to nine.

Five cosmetic containers. Top: left, Poudre por Le Bain; center, "April Showers" powder tin by Cheramy;
right, "Dulcia" powder tin by Cheramy, Paris. Bottom: left, "L'Odeur Intrigue" by Volupté bath powder
atomizer; right, "Detecto" charm box tin by Jacobs Bros., New York City. 1929. $35-100 each.

Richard Hudnut was one of the most successful companies of the Art Deco era as was Bourjois, with their "Evening in Paris" line.

Box for "Violet Sec" perfume by Richard Hudnut. Artist: M.L. Pinel.

Three jars. Belgium. 1935. "Violet Sec" box by Richard Hudnut. $15-125 each.

Left, "Chic" handkerchief box by Tootal, England. Top right, "Dubarry" face powder box, England. Bottom right, "Marvelous" eye makeup set by Richard Hudnut. $20-45 each.

Top left and bottom right, powder boxes for "Marvelous" face powder by Richard Hudnut. Top right, "Illidela" bottle. Center, box lid for "sans-gene" cologne made for Henri Bendel. New York. Bottom left, tin for Betty Lou "Perkies" cleansing pads. England. $25-100 each.

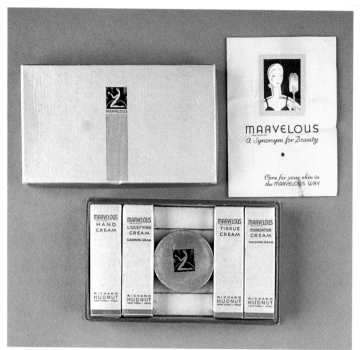

Beauty set. "Marvelous" by Richard Hudnut. $50-100.

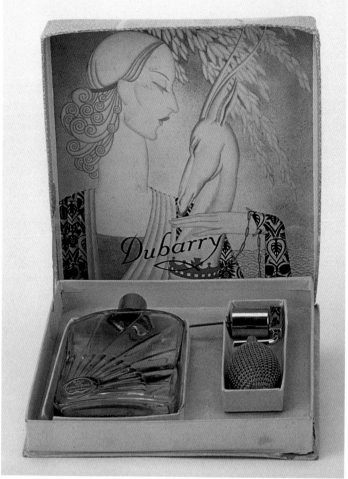

Dubarry cologne gift set. Artist: Longley. England. $125-175.

Top left, "Marvelous" makeup set by Richard Hudnut in leather box. 1937. Bottom left, brochure for set on top right. 1941. Top right, "Marvelous" makeup set in tin by Richard Hudnut. Bottom right, brochure for set on top left. $25-150 each.

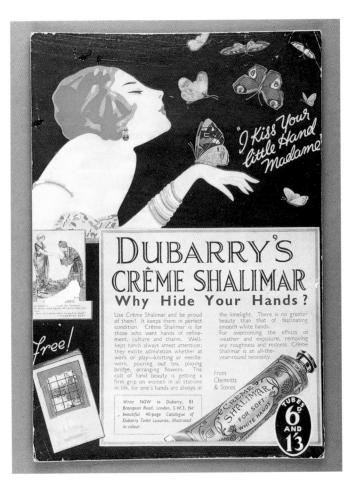

Stand up store display for Dubarry's
hand creme. England. $45-75.

Box lid for Richard Hudnut set. $35-200.

Left, box for Richard Hudnut gift set. Right, large box with satin top
for "Evening in Paris" gift set by Bourjois. 1937. $100-300 each.

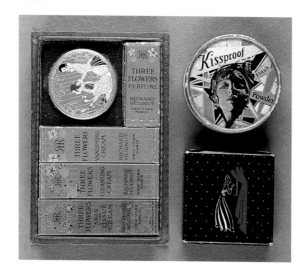

Left, "Three Flowers" Acquaintance Package by Richard Hudnut. Top right, powder box by Kissproof. Bottom right, "Evening in Paris" cardboard compact by Bourjois. 1943. $25-150 each.

Small box lid for "Evening in Paris" set by Bourjois. $50-125.

Box lid for "Evening in Paris" perfume set by Bourjois. $50-150.

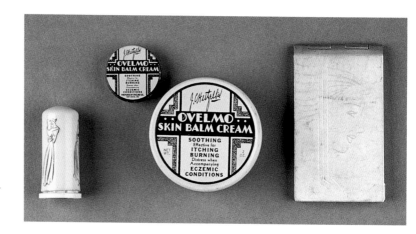

Left, "Evening in Paris" lipstick in plastic tube by Bourjois. Center, two tins for Ovelmo skin cream. Right, Metal container for Kleenex lip tissues. $15-50 each.

The selling of cosmetic gift sets at the holidays was, and still is, very popular in the cosmetic industry. The artists not only used great graphics for the boxes, but on the containers and brochures as well. The prices given are for sets.

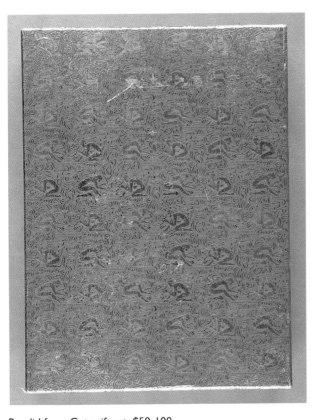

Box lid from Coty gift set. $50-100.

Mellow-glo gift set. 1928. $100-200.

Top, Box lid of Mello-glo set. Bottom left, "Maderas de Oriente" powder box by Myurgia. Artist: Eduard Jenér. Spain. Center, Tokalon metal compact. France. Right, powder tin. France. $75-200 each.

Metal box lid for Chantrey. $25-100.

Lid for Woodbury Cologne
men's gift set. $100-175.

Box lid and inside of Lioret
perfume gift set. $100-200.

Top left, Potter and Moore powder and cologne set. England. Right, inside of Yardley set. Bottom, Pond's skin freshener bottle with Bakelite top. $20-175 each.

Left, box for "Seventeen" bridge ensemble set by Colgate. Top right, booklet advertising cosmetics and compacts for the "Seventeen" line. Bottom right, "Seventeen" gun metal compact. 1931. $35-75 each.

Left, empty box. Center, Yardley vanity case set box. 1930. Right, "Illidela" fragrance in box. $15-175 each.

147

Box lid for Lander perfume gift set. $75-175.

Inside of Lander set.

The nail care industry had their own eye-catching designs and packaging. Most of these were from the Cutex Company.

Five box lids for Cutex nail kits. $15-50 each.

Five Cutex nail sets. $15-50 each.

Left, Bakelite box for Cutex nail set. Center, inside of Bakelite box. Right, Bonnet Box by Cutex nail set. $35-50 each.

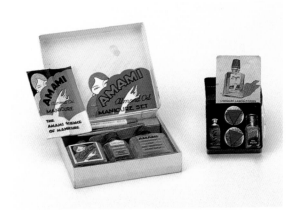

Left , Amami nail set. Right, Longlex nail set in
Bakelite box. Both England. $25-45 each.

Curling iron box by Electrex. $15-25.

Large soap label. France. $10-25.

Top left and right, box and bottle for "A Trois Cherie" by Lioret. Bottom left, Christmas box for "Djer-Kiss" perfume. Bottom right, box for "Ben Hur" perfume by Jergens. $35-65 each.

Left, box for Tokalon rouge. France. $100-200. Center and right, decorative hair pin boxes. $10-20 each.

Brochure and jar lid for "Valaze" beauty foundation cream by Helena Rubenstein. $25-45.

Top and center, Tokalon powder boxes. France. Bottom, Tokalon metal compact. $125-200 each.

Three Tokalon powder boxes.

Large cardboard store display for Plume Chiffon. $50-125.

Chapter 7
Travel

Many of the best artists of the Art Deco era designed ephemera for the travel and tourist industry. The most famous of them, such as Cassandre and Mcknight Kauffer did posters. I have not included posters in this book because the originals can be many thousands of dollars. There is, however, a lot of affordable travel paper and ephemera available today. It can be found at most flea markets in the United States and Europe, auctions, and paper shows. Items to look for are brochures put out by railroads, steamship companies, automobile companies, hotels, historic sites, and different countries. Wonderful Art Deco graphics can be found on maps, menus, luggage labels, souvenir postcards, and many other kinds of ephemera.

Even though part of the Art Deco era was during the Depression, there were people who could always afford to travel. Travel by ship was the most elegant and luxurious way to go. For most people the idea of boarding a beautiful boat with trunks of clothes was only a dream. The luxury liner "Normandie" was the epitome of excess and opulence. Built in France in 1932, the interiors were designed by the most famous and talented artists that France had to offer. Jean Dupas, Emile-Jacques Ruhlman, and René Lalique were among the many who contributed to the elegant interior design of the public rooms. Although France was not affected as much by the Depression as the United States, the luxury trades were no longer getting the large orders from British and American customers. The building of this ship gave work to a number of artists facing the economic difficulties of the time. The "Normandie" was launched in 1935 and although it was advertised as an almost totally fireproof ship, it caught fire seven years later in New York harbor, and, unfortunately, was too damaged to salvage.

In the United States, the Machine Age was gathering steam. The streamline designs by Raymond Lowey, Norman Bel Geddes, Henry Dreyfus, Walter Dorwin Teague, and others in the transportation and industrial design fields were outstanding. Sleek, smooth lines and graphics of new trains, planes, and automobiles made the rest of the world turn from France, which had been the pinnacle of style for many years, and look to the United States for ideas.

The advertising industry, using speed, sleekness, and psychology, gave the consumer a message that holds up today: "nothing is made to last." Newer, more exciting models and styles come out every year and if the people can't buy them, then something is lacking in their lives.

Another area that you can find great Art Deco graphics is World's Fair items. Some are more expensive than others, but they still can be found reasonably priced.

I have also put theater programs in this category, because most people have to travel to get to one, and it is a part of the holiday experience for a lot of people. They are easy to find and have some of the best examples of Art Deco graphics and advertising of the time.

As in the other categories, prices vary according to condition, availability, and if the piece is artist signed.

The 1933 Chicago Century of Progress was an exhibition to celebrate Chicago's 100th anniversary. Its modern and futuristic pavilions were models of Art Deco and streamline design. From the many pavilions representing American companies to the wonderful foreign exhibits, this incredible fair helped Americans forget the Depression and look ahead to the future.

The most famous World's Fair was the 1939-1940 New York World's Fair. Our best and most talented designers and artists helped make this the most successful and forward-thinking fair of the century in the United States. George Gershwin wrote a song for the opening ceremonies entitled "Dawn of a New Day." The fair and its futuristic ideas were just that for the American people. Imagine being able to go through Norman Bel Geddes's "Futurama" exhibit.

Over 25,000 types of souvenirs were made for this fair and they are still available at various markets, shops, and shows. There are, however, many World's Fair collectors who compete for objects in this area. As futuristic as the design was for the fair, most of the printed material and ephemera abound in Art Deco graphics.

The use of artists to design beautiful theater program covers was always done in London and Paris. Some regional theaters in the United States used artists like George Barbier, but Broadway theaters, except in the early part of the century, mostly used and still use the Playbill.

The travel industry from all over the world produced
large numbers of beautifully illustrated brochures and maps
for their countries.

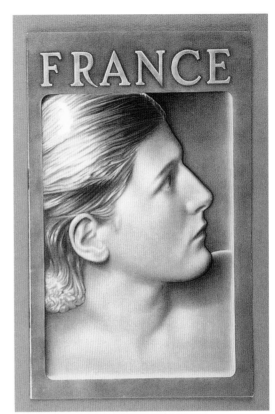

Brochure of France from the
1939 World's Fair. $10-15.

Top, bridge tally card. Buzza-Clark Company. Center, double deck of
Russell playing cards. Bottom, three playing cards. USPC.

Eight assorted travel postcard
books. France. $15-25 each.

Left, "Tourist." USPC. Center, travel brochure. France. Right, "Lumiere" film envelope. France. $10-35 each.

Cover of *L'Illustration*. 1931. France. $75-150.

Page from *L'Illustration*. Artist: Guy Sabian.

Top, two travel postcard packs. Bottom, brochure of
Deauville. Artist: R. Ansieau. 1930. France. $10-25 each.

Liquor advertising fan. Artist:
A. Ramboz. France. $25-45.

Left, French Riviera travel
brochure. Right, menu
illustration of Ceylon.
Charles Heidsieck Cham-
pagne. France. $15-45 each.

155

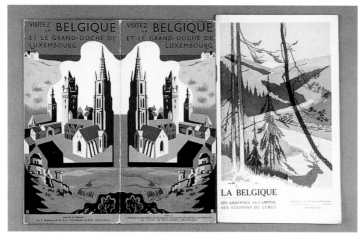

Two travel brochures. Belgium. Left, 1938. Right, 1930. $10-20 each.

Travel map of Gstaad. Switzerland. $15-25.

Two travel brochures. Switzerland. $10-20 each.

Two travel brochures. Switzerland. $10-20 each.

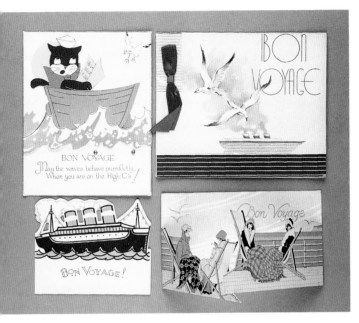

Four "Bon Voyage" cards. Top row, Rust Craft. Bottom left, Norcross. Bottom right: unmarked. $5-15 each.

Left, Jasper National Park brochure. 1928. Right, Sunoco map. 1939. $10-25 each.

Left, Toronto brochure. 1930. Right, Canadian Steamship Company brochure. 1927. $10-25 each.

Quebec brochure. $10-20.

"Greetings" telegram depicting different modes of travel. Artist: C.J. Bouttell. 1924. England. $10-25.

Top, Shakespeare Country brochure in French. Great London Railway. 1939. Bottom, Shakespeare Country brochure. 1938. England. $10-20 each.

Left, Royal Scot Railway brochure from 1933 World's Fair. Right, London
Midland and Scottish Railroad brochure. 1932. England. $10-40 each.

London Railway Brochure. 1932. London
Midland and Scottish Railway. $10-20.

Travel magazine cover. 1938. $20-35.

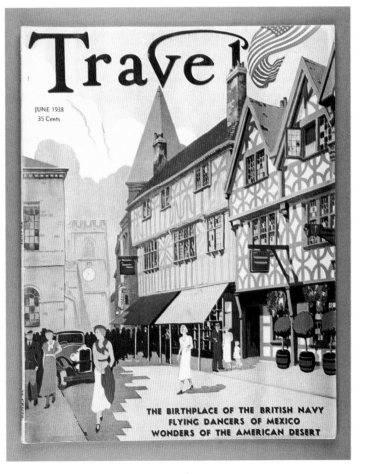

The luxury liners were the only way to travel for the
wealthy. The lucky ones got to sail on "The Normandie."

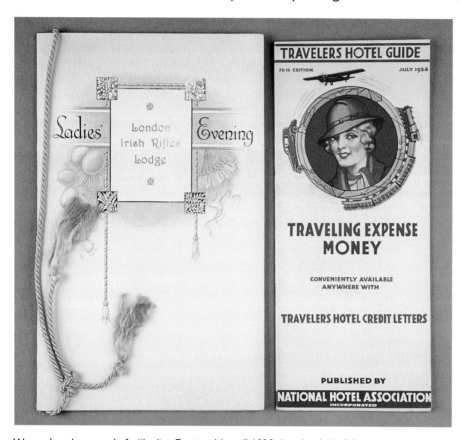

Women's ephemera. Left, "Ladies Evening Menu." 1938. London Irish Rifle Lodge.
Right, Traveler's Hotel Association Guide. 1934. United States. $15-35 each.

Apertif lablel. "Normandy" brand. France. $15-25.

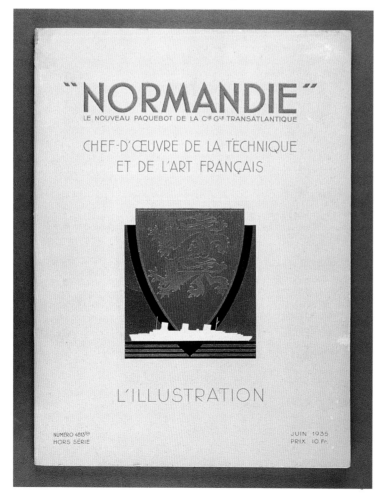

Cover of L'Illustration . "Normandie"
issue. June 1935. France. $75-200.

Illustration from *L'Illustration.*

Illustration of the swimming pool and children's area of the Normandie.

Illustration of Le Grande Salon of the Normandie from *L'Illustration.*

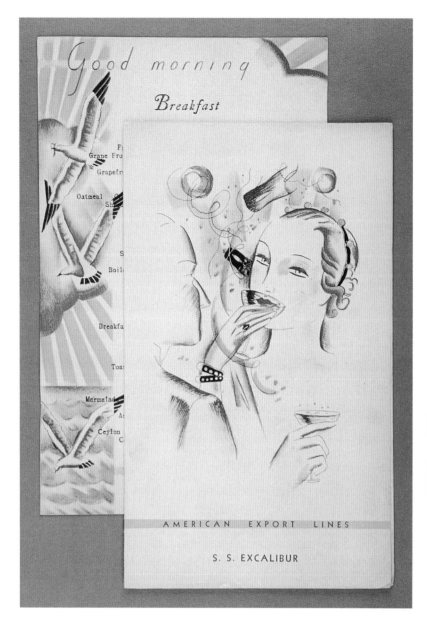

Menu from the S.S. Excalibur.

Menus from the S.S. Excalibur. 1936. American Export Lines. $10-20 each.

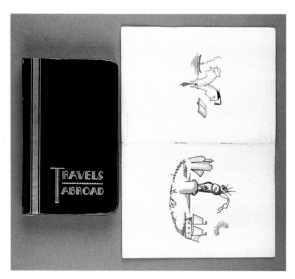

Left, travel diary. Samuel Ward, Boston. Right, passenger list from the S.S. New Amsterdam college trip. 1927. Holland America Line. $25-50 each.

Advertising fan. Red Star Line. $45-75.

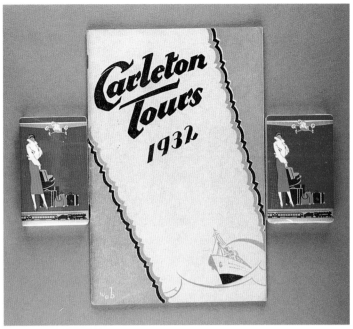

Left, passenger list from R.M.S. Carinthia. 1934. Cunard Line. Right, passenger list from the S.S. Santa Paula. 1937. Grace Line. $25-65 each.

Right and left, Russell playing cards. Center, Carleton Tours Brochure. 1932. $25-35 each.

Brochure. Students Travel Club. 1927. New York. $15-25.

Hand colored plate. $50-200.

Here is some more colorful travel ephemera, including
some from different World's Fairs.

Map of Mexico. $10-20.

Argentores cover. Bulletin of Society of
Authors. 1944. Artist: Zonome. Argentina.

Two travel brochures. Left, Venezuela. Artist:
Carter Perkins. 1933. Right, Havana. 1938.

Two brochures from 1933-34 Century of Progress Chicago World's Fair. Top, Baltimore and Ohio Railroad. Bottom, Pennsylvania Railroad. $15-35 each.

Three travel brochures of Italy. $10-15 each.

Cover *Italia* magazine. Artist: Luigi Piffero. 1939 World's Fair. $20-30.

Brochure of Greece. 1939 World's Fair. $15-25.

Two brochures of Norway. 1939 World's Fair. $15-25 each.

Two brochures of The Netherlands. 1939 World's Fair. $15-30 each.

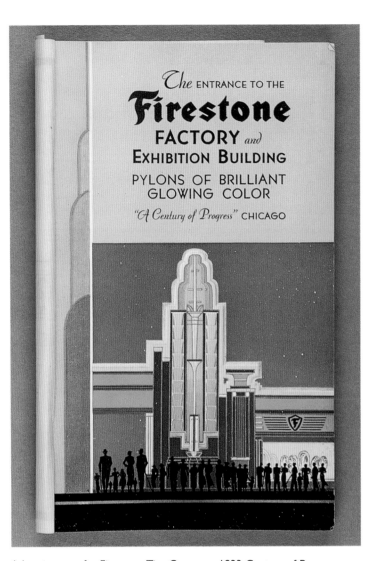

Top, Ford Motor Company brochure. 1933 Century of Progress. Center, ticket for 1933 Century of Progress. Bottom, Greyhound Bus Company, receipt for 1933 Century of Progress trip. $15-35 each.

Advertisement for Firestone Tire Company. 1933 Century of Progress.

Two travel brochures of Florida. Left, 1936. Right, 1937. $10-20 each.

Left, brochure for Chicago featuring Fanny Brice. 1934. Right, brochure of the Empire State Building. $10-20 each.

Two travel brochures. Left, Vermont. Right, Maine. $10-25 each.

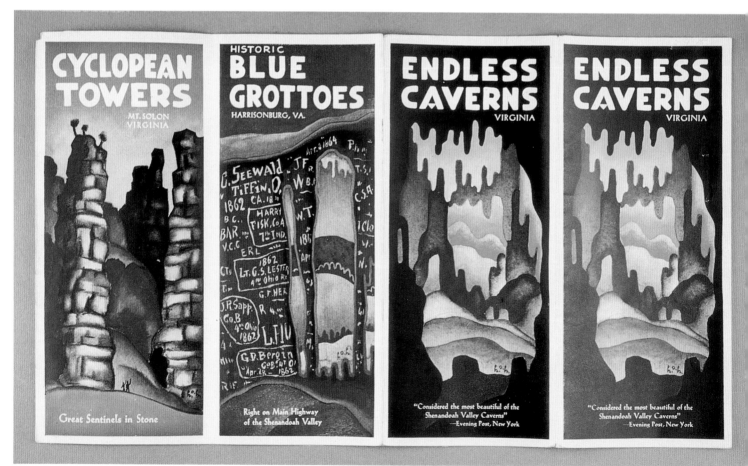

Travel brochure. Endless Caverns, Virginia. $10-20.

"Travel" Study Book. 1936.
American Education Press. $10-20.

Three postcards. Top, Hotel Traylor, Allentown, Pennsylvania.
Center, Mayfair Roof Apartment Hotel, Philadelphia. Bottom,
Atlantic City Convention Center. $5-10 each.

Sailor serving tray. $25-50.

Travel brochure of New York City. 1945. $15-25.

Theater programs from many countries were great examples of the Art Deco graphics of the time.

Three theater programs. Top left, 1932. Bottom, 1931. Right, artist: Baejansky. 1925. All France. $15-45 each.

Cover of program for "American Jubilee" at the 1940 New York World's Fair. Artist: Joseph Binder. $25-35.

Left, movie program. 1932. London. Right, theater program. 1937. Scotland. $15-45 each.

Top, program from Casino de Paris. Artist: Zig (Louis Gaudin). France. Bottom, program from Radio City Music Hall. 1941. New York City. $20-45 each.

Theater program for Prince of Wales Theater. Artist: Louis Curli. 1938. London. $25-50.

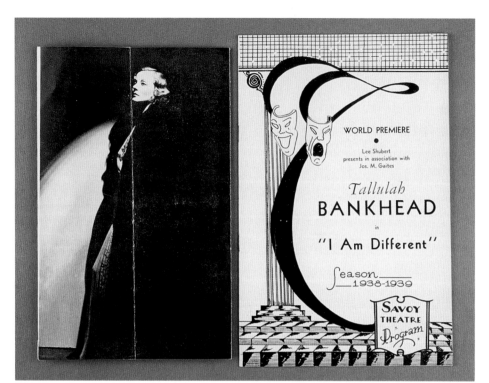

Theater program for Savoy Theater featuring Tallulah Bankhead. 1938. San Diego, California. $15-30.

Three theater programs. Top left, 1931. Artist: Pierre Brissaud. Bottom left, 1932. Right, artist: Troy. 1935. All France. $15-45 each.

Theater program for The London Palladium. 1935. $25-50.

Two theater programs. Left, 1934.
Right, 1932. Both London. $15-45 each.

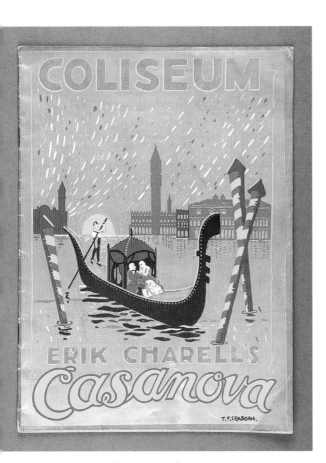

Theater program for The London Coliseum.
Artist: T.P. Seaborn. 1933. $20-50.

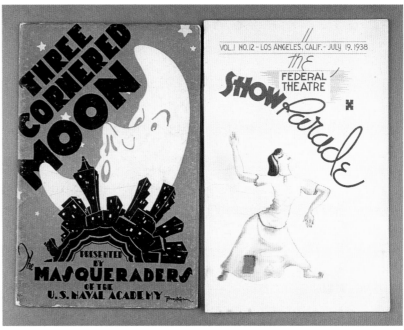

Two theater programs. Left, U.S. Naval Academy. Artist: Roben
Madison.1934. Right, 1938. Los Angeles, California. $15-35 each.b

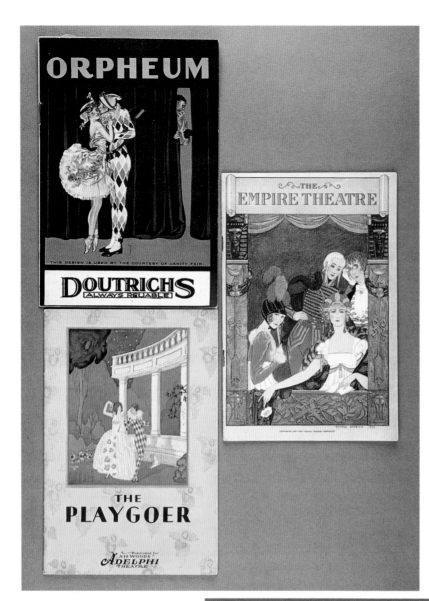

Program for The Folies Bergere. 1930. France. $50-100.

Three theater programs. Bottom left, 1928.
Right, artist: George Barbier. 1930. $25-50 each.

Two theater programs. Left,
1932. London. Right, artist:
W.D. Nichols. 1925. St. Louis,
Missouri. $15-25 each.

Bibliography

Books

Baker, Eric and Blik, Tyler. *Trademarks of the 20s and 30s*. San Francisco, California: Chronicle Books, 1985.

Battersby, Martin. *The Decorative Twenties*, ed. Phillipe Garner. New York: Whitney Library of Design, 1988.

____. *The Decorative Thirties*, ed. Phillipe Garner. New York: Whitney Library of Design, 1988.

Dodge, Edward, ed. *Encyclopedia of American Biography*. New York: American Historical Company, 1968. Vol XXXVIII, pp. 489-491.

Duncan, Alastair. *The Encyclopedia of Art Deco*. New York: E.P. Dutton, 1988.

Ercoli, Giuliano. *Art Deco Prints*. New York: Rizzoli, 1989.

Fusco, Tony. *Art Deco: Identification and Price Guide*. New York: Avon Books, 1993.

George E. Buzza obituary. *Minneapolis Sunday Tribune*. April 14, 1957, p.12B.

Gerson, Roselyn. *Vintage Ladies Compacts*. Paducah, Kentucky: Collectors Books, 1996.

Goodrum, Charles and Dalrymple, Helen. *Advertising in America: The First 200 Years*. New York: Harry N. Abrams, Inc., 1990.

Heide, Robert and Gilman, John. *Popular Art Deco*. New York: Abbeville Press, 1991.

Heller, Steven and Fili, Louise. *Streamline*. San Francisco: Chronicle Books, 1995.

____. *French Modern*. San Francisco: Chronicle Books, 1997.

____. *British Modern*. San Francisco: Chronicle Books, 1998.

Herring, Stephen. *South Middlesex- A New England Heritage*. Northridge, California: Windsor Publications, 1986.

Jones-North, Jacquelyne. *Commercial Perfume Bottles*. West Chester: Schiffer Publishing Ltd., 1987.

Jones, Sydney R. *Art and Publicity*. London: The Studio, Ltd., 1925.

Kery, Patricia Frantz. *Art Deco Graphics*. New York: Harry N. Abrams, Inc., 1986.

Lefkowith, Christie Mayer. *The Art of Perfume*. New York: Thames and Hudson, 1994.

McClinton, Katherine Morrison. *Art Deco: A Guide for Collectors*. New York: Clarkson N. Potter, Inc., 1972.

Meikle, Jeffrey L. *Twentieth Century Limited*. Philadelphia: Temple University Press, 1979.

Opie, Robert. *The 1930s Scrapbook*. London: New Cavendish Books, 1997.

Robinson, Julian. *The Golden Age of Style*. London: Orbis Publishing, 1976.

Schwartz, Lynell. *Vintage Compacts & Beauty Accessories*. Atglen, Pennsylvania: Schiffer Publishing, Ltd., 1997.

Young, Frank. *Modern Advertising Art*. New York: Covici, Friede Inc., 1930.

Company Publications

Saberson, Raymond E. *The first hundred years: a brief story of the early incidents in the history of Craftacres*. Minneapolis, 1924. pp. 49-63.

Seventy Five Years 1844-1919. Framingham, Massachusetts: The Dennison Company, 1919.

Round Robin Magazine. Framingham, Massachusetts: The Dennison Company, 1925. pp. 3-4.

Anniversary 1850-1950. Cincinnati, Ohio: The Gibson Art Co., 1950.

Our 125th Anniversary 1850-1975. Cincinnati, Ohio: Gibson Greeting Cards, Inc., 1975.

1925 Encyclopédie des arts décoratifs et industriels modernes au XXème siècle. Volumes I-XII. New York: Garland, 1977.

Index